Reading the Novel

An introduction to the techniques of interpreting fiction

Roger B. Henkle

Brown University

Harper & Row, Publishers

New York   Hagerstown   San Francisco   London

Sponsoring Editor: James B. Smith
Project Editor: Robert Ginsberg
Designer: Andrea C. Goodman
Production Supervisor: Kewal K. Sharma
Compositor: Maryland Linotype Composition Co.
Printer & Binder: The Murray Printing Company

READING THE NOVEL
An Introduction to the Techniques of Interpreting Fiction

Library of Congress Cataloging in Publication Data
Henkle, Roger B
        Reading the novel.

        Bibliography: p.
        Includes index.
            1. Fiction—Technique.   2. Criticism.
I. Title.
PN3365.H46   801'.953   77-4355
ISBN 0-06-042785-X

Acknowledgments

SAUL BELLOW. From *Henderson the Rain King*. New York: Viking Press, 1959. Copyright © 1958, 1959 by Saul Bellow. Reprinted by permission of The Viking Press.

WILLIAM FAULKNER. From *The Sound and the Fury*. New York: Random House, 1929. Copyright © 1929 renewed 1957 by William Faulkner.

F. SCOTT FITZGERALD. From *The Great Gatsby*. New York: Scribner, 1925. Copyright 1925 by Charles Scribner's Sons.

ERNEST HEMINGWAY. From *The Sun Also Rises*. New York: Scribner, 1926. Copyright 1926 by Charles Scribner's Sons.

JOHN UPDIKE. From *Rabbit, Run*. New York: Knopf, 1960. Copyright © 1960 by John Updike.

contents

Preface

My teaching experience, and that of many other teachers of fiction, has made it clear that a great many readers—including
those in college level and even graduate level fiction courses—
do not know how to go about reading a novel. We can all get the
general drift of most books, but reading a good novel critically,
fully understanding its themes, its means of influencing a reader's attitudes and values, its use of characterization, imagery,
and language, appears to be difficult for even the most widely
read. Most of us tend to read in an uncritical manner, and
sense all too often that we have missed much of the novel's
complexity and subtlety. On the other hand, literary criticism
looks, to many people, like an occult and highly intellectual operation that they will never attain. The premise of this book is that
all reasonably intelligent readers can learn to read critically, and
in the first chapter I demonstrate the methods: what to look for,
what to note down, how to make use of one's personal responses,
how to relate material. In subsequent chapters I explain the
elements of the novel—characterization, structure, scene—in
ways that are designed to assist in understanding any novel
while reading it.

This book is intended to be of use inside and outside a classroom. It is designed to apply to all serious fiction, not just to that
in a specific area or specific course. It is designed to be used as

a supplement to what is taught in courses in the novel, as a reference, or as an introduction that can be expanded upon. I have found that most works on critical reading fall into two groups: either collections of short stories or novel excerpts intended to illustrate various aspects of critical reading, or anthologies of critical articles on the novel. The former usually require that the stories or novel excerpts be taught in order to illustrate the critical issues adequately, and this invariably cramps a teacher's style. The latter are often collections of articles designed for highly sophisticated readers—the articles were, after all, written originally for critical journals.

My book avoids, I believe, the disadvantages of both these kinds of books. It can be read as a supplement to any syllabus in any period or area of the novel that the instructor chooses, and it is designed to introduce critical concepts in a way that unsophisticated students will understand. Rather than present the critical terms in an abstract manner, I have sought to demonstrate, for example, how they affect the reading experience, how they draw on our expectations about character or our likely moral responses. Each chapter uses illustrations from novels that many first year college students have read or heard about, and each is organized to give students some awareness of the sort of thing to look for when they read a novel on their own.

Some of the approaches employed and the observations made in the book have been drawn from my own teaching, reading, and study, so there is a considerable amount of original conceptual material. I have tried, however, to introduce readers to the ideas of many of those who have written on the theory and criticism of the novel, so that the book serves as a basic explanation of the issues that arise in critical reading on almost any level. I have incorporated, largely in Chapter 2, a general overview of some of the developments in the novel. And I have included a bibliography of books on the novel for readers interested in pursuing their study further. Finally, this book is designed so that it can be read straight through as an introduction, or can be used selectively as a reference of methods of reading critically. Chapter 8 is an informal checklist, containing summaries of the techniques and considerations elaborated more fully in previous chapters. Throughout, the book builds upon the central assumption of interpretation of fiction: that as the critical techniques are put to use, they yield more and more reading satisfaction.

ROGER B. HENKLE

Reading
the Novel

How to Read Novels: Taking notes· How interpretations emerge

1

THE purpose of this book is to help you become a better reader of novels. My experience in teaching fiction indicates that most people would like to become more self-confident readers; they would like to get beyond the stage in which they can only confess, "Well, I can see it when we discuss it in class, or when the professor points it out, but when I'm reading on my own I miss a lot." There is no need for such despair, for the vast majority of the best novels can be appreciated in a full way by all of us— and outside of a classroom. The key to this appreciation lies in understanding how authors manipulate and draw upon our own attitudes and responses in order to create the drama and the meanings of their novels.

In this chapter, I will suggest a technique for reading fiction in order to get the most we can from it. Every one of us is a passive reader to some extent. The temptation is to let the experience of the novel wash into our minds, knowing that much of the detail will drain right back out, but hoping that a residue of ideas and insights into human behavior will nonetheless remain. Such reading inevitably leads to dissatisfaction with ourselves, to the sneaking feeling that we are coming away from the book with only the most general, simple impressions. We sense that we have little comprehension of the levels of meaning, characterization, image, and reference which we know are important, but which we have not taken the trouble, or simply do not know how, to understand. My intention is to indicate what to look for in reading a novel: where the clues to meaning lie, how to discover and disentangle patterns, how to go about resolving apparent inconsistencies, what to make of seemingly irrelevant characters or incidents. Armed with just a few suggestions, and with some notions about the structuring and methods of the novel, you will discover that much of what you were missing in casual readings is readily accessible to you.

There are, I know, a number of readers who strongly object to critical analysis of fiction. First of all, they are irritated when a teacher or critic begins to expound all the patterns and hidden meanings that he claims to find in what seems to be a straightforward book. The minute the instructor starts to prove that the love affair of the hero and heroine is a working out of the Adam and Eve myth, or that the author secretly hates his mother, or that the characters are illustrating something called an existential dilemma, this reader wants to cry out in protest: "Aren't you reading things *into* the novel? You can't tell me that the author meant all of that." He suspects that the motive of scholarly criticism is more the critic's desire to display his own intellectual prowess than to explain the work of art. This issue—what the author intended and what we can legitimately interpret from what he said—is a vital one that I shall get back to later in this chapter.

A second objection to critical reading, though, should be faced right away. Some students fear that the *study* of fiction will ruin the reading experience itself. They assert that they turn to novels only for enjoyment, not for intellectual challenge. Why should they have to worry a book to death, they ask, running down references, image patterns, and literary devices?

It is certainly true that novels can be read without studious attention to literary concerns; many of the best novelists insist that a book should be, first of all, a good story that keeps the reader's interest. But take a novel such as Joseph Heller's *Catch-22*, which can be read for pure enjoyment; don't we wonder, no matter how relaxed our approach, why the chronology of events has been deliberately mixed up? It might actually increase our pleasure with the novel if we could see what the intentions and the effects of such a rearrangement of the action were, for we would then feel more in command of what we were observing. Similarly, it would enrich our appreciation of the novel if we could put its message into clearer perspective. Does Heller, or does our generation, approach war differently than previous generations did? Why are the characters in *Catch-22* given comic book names such as Milo Minderbinder or Major Major Major, and why are they so one-dimensional, so uncomplex, while characters in earlier novels that we have read, such as *The Red Badge of Courage*, are developed much more fully? It may not necessarily mean that Heller cannot create complicated human beings; it may be that his techniques, and his objectives, are different from Stephen Crane's. We will not know this unless we understand something about fictional characterization. Once we attain such an understanding, we shall have the added pleasure of being able to comprehend and value Heller's methods, his design for the book. The comic scenes will be no less amusing than they originally were; they will, in fact, be all the more delightful because we can now fully appreciate what we are reading.

Even if we turn to a novel for escape—to lose ourselves awhile in fantasy when life becomes too dull or crass or heavy—we will discover that the trip into imagination is more intriguing when we have become unconsciously attuned (as we will be after studying the way a novel is structured) to the manipulative devices that a good novelist uses to exploit our hidden anxieties, fears, and desires. Lewis Carroll's *Alice in Wonderland* has enjoyed a popular revival as adult escape literature in the last decade. If we understand that Carroll felt particularly oppressed by the responsibilities of being an adult, and was half-timidly experimenting in his books with the possibilities of deliberately irresponsible adult behavior—and if we are aware that the book resembles the human dream process, that the characters may personify the author's apprehensions and guilts, and that the fear of madness and anarchy shoots through the book—our excursion into Wonderland takes on greater personal significance. We are no longer passive subjects who cannot define the powers and fascinations that are gripping us. We enter the world of the mysterious and improbable, knowing what we are escaping from and what lures us on.

No matter how lightly we take our reading, then, a familiarity with the way that the novel operates upon us will add other dimensions of interest, pleasure, and even excitement. The novelist needs our personal involvement before he can achieve his best dramatic and imaginative results, because literature functions, as no other study of human relationships does, in the realm of personal responses and interactions. Fiction and drama present men and women reacting to each other in the way that is closest to real life. This is literature's great advantage over other disciplines. History, sociology, anthropology, and psychology may better enable us to isolate certain factors in human behavior, and they allow us to categorize such factors more effectively than literature does because they are more objective fields of study. In the novel, our opinions of human behavior are, admittedly, distorted by our personal, our subjective responses to the characters and sometimes to the storyteller.

Yet valuable though it is to have the perspectives on our fellow men that the social sciences can furnish us, our actual experiences will be closer to the ones we find in fiction or the drama. For we deal with someone in real life only in the context of previous associations and exchanges; we build up attitudes toward him and he to us that complicate the issues. We may find him disgusting, pathetic, lovable, or incalculably stupid. In reading the novel, we duplicate that situation.

When you and I turn, in Chapter 4 of this book, to a discussion of the point of view from which the action in fiction is seen, and to the different kinds of narrators that can be used, we will see that writers deftly control our responses to their characters. They increase the amount of emotional distortion by adjusting the lens through which we observe the world in the novel, just as any person we are talking with can shape our view of a third person by leaving out important facts or by slanting the facts. Similarly, the people in a novel's world are not isolated from the contexts of their families, friends, and enemies when we encounter them; they are caught in the web of past mistakes, desperate hopes, or uneasy relationships in which men and women in real life operate. Hence there is no more sensitive and versatile laboratory for the understanding of individual or group behavior, or for registering our own reactions, than literature.

My stress, as you can see, is upon the relationship that we as readers develop with the author and his material, and upon the means a skillful writer uses to manipulate that relationship. One of the unique characteristics of the novel as an art form is that it demands a movement in and out of the novelistic world. Sometimes we enter the book to lose ourselves in it, to take ourselves away from the everyday world of ordinary experience in which we are constantly having to make ethical decisions, having to compromise and adjust, and make allowances for the wishes or demands of other people. Some novels deliberately cut off that everyday world, as we shall see when we examine fictional forms in Chapter 2. Other novels seem to be recreating our ordinary experience, as if they were asking us to look constantly at our real lives. In both cases we have to suspend our emotions and attitudes in order to give ourselves up temporarily to the author's vision, and yet in both cases we must never lose our ability to feel and to react, for that is what shapes our experience as readers. The novel that I have chosen to use in demonstrating the techniques of reading fiction, Saul Bellow's *Henderson the Rain King*, furnishes a particularly apt illustration of the way we are compelled to shift between the novel's world and our own experience. Bellow's book is about a contemporary American who shares some of our own puzzling and unhappy aspirations and failures (but to a greater degree, for everything is always a bigger disaster when it happens to Henderson), and who yet goes through a series of strange adventures in Africa that require of us an escape into imagination.

But let us discover what we can do with *Henderson* and how it can be applied to our reading of all novels. We begin by listening to Henderson himself; he is impossible to ignore. The novel opens this way:

> What made me take this trip to Africa? There is no quick explanation. Things got worse and worse and worse and pretty soon they were too complicated.
> When I think of my condition at the age of fifty-five when I bought the ticket, all is grief. The facts begin to crowd me and soon I get a pressure in the chest. A disorderly rush begins— my parents, my wives, my girls, my children, my farm, my animals, my habits, my money, my music lessons, my drunkenness, my prejudices, my brutality, my teeth, my face, my soul! I have to cry, "No, no, get back, curse you, let me alone!" But how can they let me alone? They belong to me. They are mine. And they pile into me from all sides. It turns into chaos.
> However, the world which I thought so mighty an oppressor has removed its wrath from me. But if I am to make sense to you people and explain why I went to Africa I must face up to the facts. I might as well start with the money. I am rich. From my old man I inherited three million dollars after taxes, but I thought myself a bum and had my reasons, the main reason being that I behaved like a bum. But privately when things got very bad I often looked into books to see whether I could find some helpful words, and one day I read, "The forgiveness of sins is perpetual and righteousness first is not required." This impressed me so deeply that I went around saying it to myself. But then I forgot which book it was.

Here is a man who is trying to reach us, to make us understand the agonies that he has endured, a man trying to compel us, through the sheer force of his personality, to listen to the story of his mixed-up life. Like so many men we meet in real life who are trying to make contact with us, Henderson doesn't know how to go about it well. His appeal is disjointed, bouncing from one subject to another. And, like too many confused souls in real life, he says things that may drive away our sympathy. Only a boor would tell us, the minute we meet him, that he inherited $3 million after taxes. We instinctively recoil from people who try to impress us in that way. And what do we care if he feels "a pressure in his chest"? Why should we listen to his story about a trip to Africa? Why, in fact, should we spend our time hearing about his troubles with his animals and his teeth? His brutality and drunkenness?

Yet, in a strange way, we *do* care. We come to literature to learn about other people, and the great advantage of literature is that we can enter into the lives of people whom we would not like if we met them in the flesh: the Macbeths and Heathcliffs and Scrooges, men alien to our own experience. In Henderson's very confusion, his very crudeness, we can see the desperate appeal of a fellow human being trying to communicate with us in the only ways he knows how. So we must hold back our initial hostility and impatience, suppress our feelings awhile until we uncover more of him. But we should not disregard our responses to Henderson altogether. We are not totally unemotional and unopinionated people ourselves, after all, and Bellow must know that and must be counting upon our reactions playing some part in understanding the experiences of the book. But for now we suspend them. As I shall illustrate presently, they will prove useful in validating our interpretations of the novel. And in subsequent chapters I will show that our reactions are never completely inoperative, even when suspended.

What should we take note of, then, if we are to make the most of this encounter with Henderson? I suggest that once we have sized up the character in a preliminary way—as we have done with Henderson—we should begin to look at what he chooses to talk about. His money, of course, his age (55), his sense of the confusion of his life ("It turns to chaos"), his search for the meaning of life ("I often looked in books to see whether I could find some helpful words"), and his attempt to find solace in Biblical phrases (" 'The forgiveness of sins is perpetual' "). These are not only clues to Henderson's personality and outlook, but probably keys to the novel's meaning. One of the tricks of critical analysis is to note the *unusual* or *striking* things that are included in the book. Many experienced readers of fiction jot down, in margins or on separate sheets of paper, some of these unusual characteristics. By this method one can focus on aspects of a character or situation that one might otherwise pass up. Surely we will not want to note everything; that is boring and defeats the purpose of selecting only the striking things. And if we do this with every book we read we also may, as some readers fear, kill the joy of a book. But I recommend that you take notes on a few novels, especially if you are reading them for a course, and you will soon discover that the note-taking procedure itself starts you thinking about the novel in a more analytical way. Once you have done this with several novels, you will find that your attention gravitates toward material that may be useful for interpretation.

Notes on the basic plot or on the major lines of action will *not* help you particularly, however, except in novels where the course of action is deliberately confused. Too often people who are beginning the study of literature assume that analysis of a novel means telling the plot over again in their own words. There is no point in that by itself; any halfway intelligent reader can grasp the basic plot outlines of most novels. Attention to the main line of action in a novel is important in that it is often through manipulation of our expectations as to what will happen in the novel that the author directs us toward the insights and meanings he wants us to grasp; but, as we will discuss in Chapter 3, this requires of us only that we stop occasionally and ask questions about what we anticipate the form of a particular novel to be. Note how quickly, for instance, you can make assumptions about the structure of *Henderson* from the opening lines alone. First of all, you assume that the novel will deal with Henderson's trip to Africa. "What made me take this trip to Africa?" In addition, you have a number of indications that Henderson is talking not just about one event, but about a series of crucial events that may possibly account for the mess that he says he has made of his life. You can project from this, and from his remark that he often turned to books to "find some helpful words," that this novel will be about his search for identity or stability and the possible solutions he found. Remarkably, you have almost unconsciously anticipated the kinds of events that will make up the plot of the novel (those events in Henderson's life which so confused and oppressed him; plus a trip to Africa and what takes place there), even though you do not know yet what the specific events will be. Secondly, you have sketched out in your mind the rough outlines of a theme to the novel—Henderson's search for meaning or happiness. This will help, obviously, in selecting what to note down as you read.

It is wise, though, not to narrow the scope of your notes just to those that seem to deal with the theme. For one thing, you may not have figured out the real theme; for another, good writers work out such issues in complex, ambiguous ways. So note anything that relates to the anticipated theme and also anything that seems to put your projections in question. Keep free and open, however, because it is the material that strikes you as being odd, as being hard to fit into any pattern, that is often crucial to an honest interpretation of the novel. This is why you should pay special attention to unusual or striking aspects of the book.

In the first few pages of the novel, for instance, one can observe strange incidents having to do with death. Henderson tells us that he took fiendish delight in tormenting his first wife, Lily, by threatening suicide with a pistol. Lily's father had shot himself, so Henderson's sadistic game caused her special anguish. Yet Henderson himself has a desperate desire to get in touch with his own dead father, and in one memorable scene he passionately plays the violin in his cellar in an attempt to reach his father through the music. He cannot convince himself, he confesses, that the dead are really dead. Over and over again he asserts that he is "familiar" with death; even the sight of an octopus in an aquarium gives him "notice" of death. Odd vignettes these are, apparently establishing a pattern relating to death, but nothing that we can figure out at this point.

Henderson makes very little more sense of his family life. In one odd incident his teenaged daughter adopts a black baby. Henderson takes it away from her, as he must, and observes that he felt like pharaoh doing it—and then, apropos of nothing, he reflects that there is a curse on America. In Chapter 3, he starts to tell us his reasons for going to Africa, but suddenly breaks off to talk about his father and then, just as abruptly, switches off that topic to rail about the stealing of America's land from the Indian. What can we make of this? Apparently Henderson thinks that his personal troubles have something to do with certain evils of American culture, but he cannot make sense of it for us, and all we can do as readers is take note of it for later consideration. Not only must we pay attention to all the apparently incidental or inconsistent aspects of a book that we previously might have simply tried to ignore, but we must collect them for later analysis, with the patience and coolness of a Sherlock Holmes—or a literary critic.

At last we do get to Africa, where Henderson, in some half-conceived quest, plunges deeper and deeper into the darkest, least civilized regions. Is it emotional richness and inspiration that he seeks? Apparently not, for though he is occasionally moved to aesthetic appreciation (he knows when he has achieved it, because he contends that the apprehension of grand, beautiful things makes his teeth itch), such a feeling never lasts long; he cannot seem to hold onto it. Is it spiritual purity that he seeks? At one point he does claim to want "things that were of old, which I had when I was innocent and have longed for ever since." Whatever it is that he searches for, he is driven on by an inner voice continually crying out, "I want! I want!"

Here I would like to make another important point about note taking. As you can see, I am asking questions as I go along in an effort to reach some sort of definition of Henderson's problems and of the object of his quest. Often it is not enough to note the odd or the thematically significant incidents if one does not try to figure out what they mean. Write down questions that probe toward meaning as you go along. Even more important, try to *define* what a character's position, attitude, or objective is. Search for words such as "spiritual purity," or "maturity," or "aesthetic appreciation," or "egotistical," or "fear of death," as you take notes and use them as guidelines for interpretation. Proposing definitions in this way forces you to stop and think about what you have read and noted. It compels you to make sense of it as you go along, to wrestle with your impressions until they yield meaning. It may be useful at times to compose a sort of memorandum to yourself—to think things through on paper. For example, a paragraph of notes like this would be useful: "Henderson keeps saying 'I want!' It means he hasn't found what he's looking for. It might show how selfish and egotistical he is. Or how incomplete his life is. What does he want? More wealth? Love? Happiness? Self-respect?" This represents the vital effort of a reader struggling toward clarification, trying on various theories and defining words to see if any of them fit. It is the effort of a reader who is generating thought. Writing down the relevant questions, and trying then to reach a definition, focuses one's thinking, and refines it.

Henderson, meanwhile, bumbles on and on through the Dark Continent's most primitive reaches, forever attempting the one act that will justify him and give him comfort. He cannot refrain from doing things, no matter where he is, and in one ludicrous adventure, when he is trying to drive frogs out of a tribal cistern, he instead demolishes the dam that holds the community's entire water supply. While watching the ceremonies of another tribe, Henderson volunteers, because he is an unusually large and strong man, to perform a feat of strength that no other human had ever accomplished, moving a gigantic stone statue called the "Mummah." Henderson does lift the Mummah; at last he seems to be able to rejoice in having done something unique, even though the strain has brought him oppressive chest pains and a strange fever. The act of raising the Mummah, in fact, makes Henderson the tribe's Rain King, for miraculously the clouds open up on the long-parched land. In celebration, the natives dunk him in a mud puddle, and he describes himself as looking like a giant turnip.

How can you help but feel some compassion for a man like that, a self-styled giant turnip? We begin to pull for Henderson, who, though now a Rain King, is still so pathetically devoid of self-direction. He puts himself in the hands of a newfound friend, Dahfu, the young king of the tribe. It is an excruciating experience, for Dahfu has partially tamed a full-grown female lion, and he tries to convince Henderson that only through exposure to the danger of coming face to face, unarmed, with the lioness can he conquer the fear of death. Henderson, half believes, at times, that he is himself fulfilling the prophecy of Daniel to King Nebuchadnezzar in the Bible that "They shall drive thee from among men, and thy dwelling shall be with the beasts of the field." There are in fact, if we trace them out, some intriguing parallels to the Biblical episodes from the Book of Daniel. Nebuchadnezzar was, as Henderson is, a man born into riches who was spared the consequences of some of his own foibles and of plots against him by having his dreams interpreted by the prophet Daniel. Daniel, as almost everyone knows, was befriended by a lion, just as is Dahfu. Earlier Henderson had described his trip to Africa as being "like a dream," and we, surely, are trying to interpret it, almost as Daniel was.

The parallels with the Biblical story seem to end there. It is well to remember that Biblical parables and stories, Greek myths, and old legends, though frequently alluded to in modern fiction, are rarely worked out fully in such novels, and, though they often contribute to the novel's meaning, they are rarely statements of the novel's themes in themselves. In the case of *Henderson the Rain King*, the most trenchant question we should perhaps ask ourselves about the allusions to the Book of Daniel is what guides to happiness or self-respect or to the meaning of life does the Old Testament offer us, since we have identified the search for such guides as one of the themes of Bellow's novel.

Dahfu, the man to whom Henderson has turned for guidance, has his own agonizing challenges before him. Though

Dahfu has been educated in Europe, and would presumably be critical of superstitions, he has committed himself to capturing a wild lion which, according to tribal legend, contains the soul of his dead father. If Dahfu fails to capture the lion, he will be put to death. Therefore, Dahfu himself, for all his education and vision, is condemned to live or die by the dictates of primitime myth. The contrast between cultures is even more complex because Henderson persists in trying to explain himself to Dahfu (and to us) by harking back to America. As ever, Henderson's observations combine the perceptive and the banal:

> You have to think about white Protestantism and the
> Constitution and the Civil War and capitalism and winning
> the West. All the major tasks and the big conquests were done
> before my time. That left the biggest problem of all, which was
> to encounter death. We've just got to do something about it.
> It isn't just me. . . . I can swear to you . . . there are guys
> exactly like me in India and in China and South America and
> all over the place. Just before I left home I saw an interview
> in the paper with a piano teacher from Muncie who became
> a Buddhist monk in Burma. You see, that's what I mean.

It is hard to believe that a mind so disjointed and apparently so trivial could ever sort things out for itself, yet by the end of the book, as Henderson leaves Africa after Dahfu has been destroyed by the lion he sought to capture, Henderson has apparently found some stability. He himself defines it as reconciliation to the rhythm of life. In the last scene of the novel, Henderson cavorts with hysterical energy on the runway of an airport in Newfoundland with a lion cub and an orphaned Arab boy he has befriended; he is full of the joy of life again.

No synopsis, especially one this selective, can do credit to Bellow's novel, but we do have, at least, some notes to begin to work with in moving toward an interpretation of the novel. We know, as I have said, that Henderson has become adjusted to life in some way, but we will search in vain, I think, for an explanation of it in explicit terms. Hence our understanding of his experience is only of the vaguest kind, and we are, if we stop now, left among the ruins of conflicting possibilities, unresolved issues, frustrating digressions, and aggravating irrelevancies. We are no better able to explain what we have read than Henderson is to make sense of his own ideas and experiences.

Now those notes that we have been taking of unusual or striking matter must come through for us. We should begin by reading back through them fairly rapidly, and by trying to assemble them in some sort of related categories or complexes of ideas. For instance, we might write these things down: reconciliation to the rhythm of life, death references, Old Testament attitudes toward life, middle age (Henderson is 55), attempts (by Henderson and Dahfu) to bring back the spirits of dead fathers. Now we can only mull over these jottings, as a detective mulls over clues, and see how they might be interrelated. They do all seem to suggest that Henderson has reached that point in life when he must adjust himself to middle age and to the inevitability that he, like his father before him, will die. The Old Testament has a certain kind of tough honesty about the human condition; it asks that we be able to face aging and death with fortitude. If we have read Bellow before, or novels by other contemporary Jewish writers, we will be conscious of the recurrent theme in their fiction of acceptance of the rhythm of human life; that the sons succeed the fathers, and that it is futile to thrash about in resistance to the cycle of aging and decline, as Americans are wont to do.

Having put together a possible interpretation of the novel, we must now try to see what other items in our notes fit it, for this is one of the ways in which we can validate our interpretation. The temptation at this stage is to say, "Aha! I've got it!" and begin to collect everything that does correspond and reject or distort everything that doesn't. So the burden is upon us, as critical readers, to be as honest as we can (to avoid falling into that trap of self-serving distortion of which we think some critics and teachers to be occasionally guilty). But criticism is also a creative activity, and it requires of us a willingness to range freely through our own experience and knowledge to find usable ideas—to find postulates, as scientists do. Here we might, for example, be able to apply the common knowledge that most of us have about the nature of heart attacks: that it is the most common middle-age phenomenon, after all, that forces men to come to terms with the possibility of their own deaths. Remember that Henderson mentioned the pressure in his chest in the first page of the book, that death once gave him "notice" in the form of an octopus, that lifting the Mummah brought tightness to his chest, and that he suffered fever and loss of strength after that. In his trip out of Africa, Henderson, debilitated by a strange malady, nearly died, and was forced to make a long recuperation. Perhaps he has suffered a heart attack, and *this* experience has compelled reconciliation with life. Perhaps, indeed, the trip to Africa is only a delirious dream during the attack, so that we are closer than we thought to Daniel, who interpreted Nebuchadnezzar's dream. The plot, as they say, thickens—but this time with complexity and meaning.

Exciting though these discoveries are, they still leave some annoying inconsistencies. For one thing, if Bellow is trying to transmit to us the serious, indeed somber, experience of coming to terms with growing older, why has he chosen Henderson as his narrator and chief actor? Such a poignant theme would seem to call for a more appealing narration, not a book full of ludicrously haphazard observations on life and absurd events. Even if we have successfully repressed our initial dislike of Henderson's crudeness, even if we have come to be rather fond of the big turnip, we still wonder why Bellow chose to focus on such a self-centered and inarticulate man. Here is where our own responses to fictional characters will be useful, for they, too, must be used to validate our interpretations of a novel; they are nagging barbs at the back of the mind, telling us "You can't take that seriously" or "That doesn't make sense."

And we have other aspects of the novel in our notes that we have not satisfactorily fitted in. The emphasis Henderson puts on being rich, for example. Or his observations on America: that there is a curse on our country, that the only American task left is "doing something" about death. We noted at one point his crude observations on beauty, how it passes too quickly with just an itching in the teeth. And we noted his grand statements about searching for innocence in Africa. Finally, we remarked upon his compulsive inner cry "I want! I want!", which implies that he seeks the possession of objects; yet we also have evidence of his willingness to sacrifice all wealth and safety and possessions to *do* something grand and significant. All these may be dismissible as the disordered rantings of a man who has not yet come to terms with life, but they also seem to be almost parodies of traits that we characteristically associate with Americans. Isn't it typically American to try to "do something about" death—using the good old American know-how? Something like becoming a doctor, as Henderson plans toward the end of the novel? Doesn't it sound like our practical, no-nonsense attitude to say that beauty and inspiration are fine but don't last long enough? Haven't countless sociologists talked about the American quest for innocence? You do not have to agree with all these formulations to see that Bellow has added another dimension to his novel, a dimension that explains the character of Henderson as a kind of larger-than-life American prototype: rich, strong, lucky, and miserable. This dimension parodies aspects of the

American life-style. The piano teacher from Muncie is not the only one these days who is plunging into Buddhism for the answers to life.

If we have read very many American novels of the fifties and sixties, we will know that one of the recent trends is "apocalyptic fiction," that is, fiction which portrays American society as on the verge of destroying itself and the world around it. *Catch-22*, Kurt Vonnegut, Jr.'s *Slaughterhouse Five*, and Thomas Pynchon's *V* are examples of books dealing with the theme. There are many more, and Bellow may find them an unhealthy, self-pitying phenomenon. The observations of the chief character of another novel, *Herzog*, may be drawing Bellow's own point: "Safe, comfortable people playing at crisis, alienation, apocalypse and desperation, make me sick. We must get it out of our head that this is a doomed time, that we are waiting for the end. We love apocalypses too much, and crisis ethics and florid extremism with all its thrilling language." (The Biblical Book of Daniel, is, by the way, considered to be an apocalyptic book of the Old Testament.) So *Henderson* may be a spoof on modern apocalyptic fiction, as well as a serious statement about acceptance of life.

We may not all have known about, and seen the relevance of, Bellow's position toward apocalyptic novels, but almost any of us could have perceived the problems that would come from a totally somber reading of the novel. Our own responses seemed to rebel against it and demand another explanation. Even if our explanation is only that it appears that this book treats supposedly typical American concepts ironically, we would have come closer to a balanced reading of the novel. Previous reading of fiction, in which such play upon prevailing cultural attitudes is fairly common, would fortify this conclusion. The beauty of the study of fiction is that it is cumulative; what we have observed in one book can often help us understand another book— but only if we have read each of them as shrewdly as we tried to read *Henderson*. The moral of Henderson's own messed-up, self-indulgent life, in fact, is that wisdom does not come easy; it is not as a thing that one inherits, as were the $3 million after taxes.

To review the method I have been suggesting, then: First, ask yourself from time to time what you think the book is likely to be about, what you expect its pattern to be (more on how to do that in Chapter 4). Second, note your personal responses to the narrator (the storyteller), and to the main characters, but hold back any final judgments of them. Third, note down, in margins or on pieces of paper, unusual or striking things that are said or done or referred to. Note especially the inconsistencies, but don't be discouraged if you cannot resolve them right away. (Some of them, in fact, you may never resolve in first readings.) After you have read the novel, ask yourself again what the pattern of the work seems to be, whether it turned out to be what you earlier had anticipated. Review your notes, trying to assemble them in categories, trying to relate the aspects that seem to fit together, ignoring for the time being anything inconsistent. Once you have postulated a possible interpretation of the experiences in the novel, try to relate to it the imagery, or the references (such as those in *Henderson* to the Old Testament), or the content of minor scenes. Then validate your interpretation in two ways: First by trying to accommodate apparent inconsistencies with your reading of the novel, and second by asking if the reading squares with your own response to the characters and their experience, or with your sense of the book. Here you must be creative, but not dishonest with yourself, in handling contradictions. If you cannot reconcile your interpretations and the material of the book to your satisfaction, it may be that your interpretation is off base and that you need to go back over your notes in search of a new reading of the novel. In later chapters I will suggest to you some approaches that you can take to novel form and characterization that will make all of this less a hit-or-miss operation, but the key to critical reading—to understanding a work of fiction—lies in a procedure that notes striking material, postulates patterns and themes, and validates one's tentative conclusions.

What will come to you as you do this is the immense excitement that critical understanding can bring. Like a man working an intellectual puzzle, you will struggle with this piece or that, turning it around to see how it might fit, discarding some and picking up new ones, even quitting in frustration at times and returning to it later. Suddenly it will all come to you and you will hastily, enthusiastically, begin to connect things. Unlike a puzzle, though, some of the pieces are from your own experience, your past reading, or your own imagination, so it is to that extent a creative, not a mechanical operation. Often that flash of insight will come before you even finish the novel, because the very process of writing down notes gets your mind working on the problem unconsciously. And since most good novels intend to leave the reader conscious of ambiguity, and since language and human behavior are evocative, no previous critic will have fully analyzed a good novel, none will have gotten exactly what you can get out of it.

Most good critics follow, with their own variations, the procedure I have suggested. David Lodge, a novelist and highly respected critic, describes a similar process and its excitement:

> One seeks all the time to define what kind of novel it is, and how successful it is. . . . Constantly one makes notes (which may be mental or written) about local detail: *this* is significant or irrelevant—*this* works or doesn't work—*this* connects with or contradicts *that*. Such notes are necessarily provisional, particularly in the early stages. . . . The novel unfolds in our memories like a piece of cloth woven upon a loom, and the more complicated the pattern the more difficult and protracted will be the process of perceiving it. But that is what we seek, the pattern. . . .
>
> It is my own experience that the moment of perceiving the pattern is sudden and unexpected. All the time one has been making the tiny provisional notes, measuring each against one's developing awareness of the whole, storing them up in the blind hope that they will prove useful, and then suddenly one such small local observation sends a shock like an electric charge through all the discrete observations heaped up on all sides, so that with an exciting clatter and rattle they fly about and arrange themselves in a certain meaningful order.[1]

The method, then, works for all of us, and it works for all novels of some complexity and quality. In fact, a distinguishing characteristic of first-rate fiction is that it yields increasing riches in interpretation as you dig deeper into it. (The British critic C. S. Lewis even argues that the criterion for determining what a "good book" is should be whether it stimulates creative and analytical reading in a good—that is, attentive and sensitive— reader.) Complexity in itself does not make one novel better than another, but good novelists do take more care in making minor and apparently out-of-place incidents or references enlarge upon the meaning of the book. The method is useful for novels of almost all periods. Look, for instance, at these few paragraphs from the first page (in my edition) of Jane Austen's *Emma*, a novel published in 1816:

> Emma Woodhouse, handsome, clever, and rich, with a comfortable home and happy disposition, seemed to unite some of the best blessings of existence; and had lived nearly twenty-one years in the world wtih very little to distress or vex her.

[1] *Language of Fiction* (New York: Columbia University Press, 1966), pp. 80–81.

> She was the youngest of the two daughters of a most affectionate, indulgent father, and had, in consequence of her sister's marriage, been mistress of his house from a very early period. Her mother had died too long ago for her to have more than an indistinct remembrance of her caresses.
>
> . . .
>
> The real evils indeed of Emma's situation were the power of having rather too much her own way, and a disposition to think a little too well of herself; these were the disadvantages which threatened alloy to her many enjoyments. The danger, however, was at present so unperceived, that they did not by any means rank as misfortunes with her.

Jane Austen's narrator, more than those of modern novelists, tends to comment on her characters, so some of their important characteristics are drawn directly to our attention; but if you have read *Emma*, or Jane Austen's *Pride and Prejudice*, you know that much of what we would like to know about the characters' emotions and opinions is withheld from us until late in the book, and that the chief characters are remarkably complex human beings. It is just as essential, then, to take note of what attracts our attention in these opening paragraphs. It is perhaps even more vital in reading Jane Austen because she has the habit of telling us an important fact (such as that "the real evils indeed of Emma's situation were the power of having rather too much her own way, and a disposition to think a little too well of herself"), then throwing us off guard (as by saying that the danger was at present unperceived), then turning, as she does in the next paragraph, to a different matter altogether. We will tend to lose all these crucial observations if we do not note them somehow, and we will be blind to all the clues to Emma's misjudgments as we read along. Similarly, were we to remark to ourselves upon Emma's lack of strong parental authority (for her father proves to be childlike and senile), we might have discovered that first somewhat unusual or striking circumstance which would explain her later behavior and be a key to some of the interpretations that have been made of the novel.

We have not the space here to carry through with *Emma* even as sketchy an analysis as we gave *Henderson the Rain King*. My purpose is simply to encourage you to use the procedure we have been talking about on all good fiction. There is sometimes a tendency to think that novelists of the eighteenth and nineteenth centuries, who wrote in a presumably more leisurely time and sometimes wrote to meet certain length requirements, need not be read as carefully as modern novelists. Nobody says this about Jane Austen, but some people do say it about Charles Dickens, for instance. They argue that there are large chunks of a Dickens novel that are fillers or that are incidental to the main theme, and that to try to use them as bases of interpretation would be fruitless or would cause us to distort the work. This interpretation causes such people to miss much that is important in Dickens.

This brings us to the objection to critical analysis of fiction that I first mentioned and have put off dealing with: "Aren't we reading a lot into the book that isn't there?" "Did the author intend all that?" These are separate questions. The first is the more easily dealt with. If the basis for our interpretation is not really there, we should be able to determine that by the processes of validation that we go through. If we discover in the text passages inconsistent with our theory and we cannot reconcile them satisfactorily, then perhaps we did get carried away in our analysis. If we find, on the other hand, after careful, honest reading, some support for our interpretation of a character's behavior or attitude, and some support for a different interpretation, it is possible that the author meant to leave that behavior or attitude ambiguous—or that the character changed in the course of his experience in the novel—and we should allow for that. Human beings are notoriously ambivalent and changeable, and literature's strength, as I have said, is its ability to present people in their real complexity. To determine, in that case, whether such inconsistency means false reading on our part, or intended ambiguity on the author's part, we probably have to fall back on our own sense of the character and the situation, just as we have to when judging people's motives in real life. It is all a bit slippery (as in real life), but it is not quite as unsystematic and fanciful an operation as those skeptical of literary analysis (usually people who have never worked hard at understanding a novel) would lead us to believe.

The other question—did the author intend all that—is a trickier one. First of all, in many cases we may not need to answer that in our reading process. Art by its very nature seeks to open us up to our own responses to language, to scenes of action, to ways of behaving. This is part of the immortality of great art: that it speaks to many people in many ways. Dickens never heard of the modern concept of alienation—a feeling that one does not belong to one's world or to any of the people or things in it—that many modern critics use in order to interpret his novels, but Dickens wrote about men and women who behaved as though they were alienated, and it is valid for us to talk about them in these, our own terms. For the same reasons, the contemporary theater companies that give Shakespeare's *Hamlet* a Freudian interpretation have a certain justification for it even though the psychological concepts of Shakespeare's time are radically different from those of Freud. There are constants in human nature that enable literature to speak to various ages. So long as we do not distort the work of art, we can engage in this kind of analysis—although clearly it would be more rewarding to learn of Shakespeare's notions of psychology, since we can in that way understand what *he* was really saying as well as register what his work now signifies to us.

Novelists very rarely articulate in essays or diaries what it was that they intended in their fiction: if they could do that, they probably would not have written the novel. Therefore, understanding fiction requires that we interpret the texts ourselves, guided by our sense and honesty and aided by the richness of our own minds. In fact, many authors who describe their own creative process say that the direction of a novel, its meaning, its controlling symbol or myths, come to them almost unconsciously. The American novelist Andrew Lytle has extensively reconstructed the stages of writing a novel, and tells us that, at various points in the creation, the characters, in the "stress of the situation," took on a life of their own; that his original concept of the subject gradually became subsumed in a larger subject which had been lying in his unconscious but "painfully and haltingly" moving the novel in its direction. There are numerous accounts by writers of characters seeming to come alive, of unconscious inspirations directing the writing, and of unanticipated insights coming to the surface. The French novelist André Gide is quoted as saying that a writer can "hardly discover his intentions until he has completed his work, and perhaps not even then."[2]

So there is creative interpretative work for us to do on fiction, discoveries for us to make, once we begin to read novels carefully and shrewdly. In the next chapters, I will suggest other approaches that will help you along the way.

[2] Albert J. Guerard, "Introduction to the Issue 'Perspectives on the Novel,' " *Daedalus*, 92 (Spring 1963), 201–202.

Kinds of Novels:
Contemporary society·The last day of a mind·London brutality

2

OUR objective in this book is to develop an awareness of the elements of the novel so that one can read with fuller, richer understanding. Thus, although contentious and torrid debates rage among professional critics over such questions as "When is a novel not a novel?" and "What is the ideal form of the novel?" our approach to differences in the form of novels should be: "How does the form tell us what to look for in a novel?"

In this chapter, I will introduce you to different *kinds* of novels, and briefly explain their historical significance. My objective is to demonstrate that by identifying a novel's kind, you can make a good estimate of the sort of issues that novel is dealing with. Some novels emphasize the pattern of one person's thoughts and sensibilities;·others seem to concern themselves with the nature of a society, or with a philosophic idea. Some novels are realistic, creating complex, lifelike characters, while others develop an internal atmosphere that is uncanny, not quite right. We are engaged in futility if we approach all novels in the same way, expecting to find the same things emphasized. If a character, for instance, is not supposed to be complex and lifelike, if he is supposed to represent an idea, then it is useless to look for psychological subtlety in his portrait. If a novel's world is supposed to be bizarre and dreamlike, how can we expect to discover in it an accurate picture of the social manners of the times? Thus, we must know the *mode* of a novel, if we are to know how to proceed to interpret it. (I use the term "mode," which speaks of method and the way material is presented, rather than the term "form," which normally denotes structure and shape.) By looking at the content and manner of a work of fiction, we can go on to predict what the novel's concerns and aims are likely to be.

Let me propose four basic modes of novels: (1) the social novel, (2) the psychological novel, (3) the novel of symbolic action, and (4) the modern romance. Like everything else in literature, the categories are almost never pure. We can say, though, that most books fall primarily into one mode or another.

When we think generally about the novel, most of us have in mind the traditional novels of the nineteenth century, such as those of Dickens or Hardy or Tolstoy or Balzac or Melville— big books that describe entire societies, have varied casts of characters, are filled with action, and depict life over a period of time. These are novels that seem realistic, recreating a world resembling ours and with people much like us. The great majority of novels that have been written over the past 200 years fit that general description and fall into the mode of the *social novel*. The social novel presents lifelike characters in recognizable, probable social situations.

Let me use a recent novel, John Updike's *Rabbit, Run*, to illustrate the mode of the social novel. *Rabbit, Run* deals with a series of crises in the life of a young man named "Rabbit" Angstrom, who lives in Brewer, a medium-size town in Pennsylvania. It opens, as most social novels do, with a recognizable scene: "Boys are playing basketball around a telephone pole with a backboard bolted to it. Legs, shouts. The scrape and snap of Keds on loose alley pebbles seems to catapult their voices high into the moist March air blue above the wires. Rabbit Angstrom, coming up the alley in a business suit, stops and watches, though he's twenty-six and six three." One of the first things we notice about a novel of this sort is that it presents a great deal of specific detail about place. We are thrown into a situation or a scene that we can visualize easily and that is probably familiar to us. Social novels impart a strong sense of place through detailed descriptions of rooms, houses, countrysides, town streets and buildings, and characteristic sounds and activities. The objective is to give us enough data to project ourselves into the world being described, to understand its nature with somewhat the specificity with which we understand our own world.

A short way into *Rabbit, Run*, the protagonist, Rabbit Angstrom, whose frustrations and dissatisfactions with his life are already apparent to the reader, gets in his car and starts driving, in a characteristic American impulse to get away from it all.

> He heads down Jackson to where it runs obliquely into Central, which is also 422 to Philadelphia. STOP. He doesn't want to go to Philadelphia but the road broadens on the edge of town beyond the electric-power station and the only other choice is to go back through Mt. Judge around the mountain into the thick of Brewer and the suppertime traffic. He doesn't intend to ever see Brewer again, that flowerpot city. The highway turns from three-lane to four-lane and there is no danger of hitting another car; they all run along together like sticks on a stream. Rabbit turns on the radio. After a hum a beautiful Negress sings, "Without a song, the dahay would nehever end, without a song." Rabbit wishes for a cigarette. . . .

A passage of such specific detail gives the reader something of the texture of American life: the romance of "hitting the road," the feeling of freedom in the fast, smooth movement of a car heading out, the impersonality of a highway of automobiles like "sticks in a stream." Radio and pop music reflect an essential element of modern American life; we do, after all, tend to envelop ourselves in sound. One acquires from the novel a concrete sense of what it is like to live in contemporary America. The social novel establishes an atmosphere of reality; it plunges us into a particularized world. This is one of its identifying characteristics, whether we are speaking of Jane Austen's eighteenth-century England, Thomas Mann's middle-class Germany, or Tolstoy's St. Petersburg.

A second such characteristic is social context. A society involves a variety of people of different occupations, ages, and natures, living together in a way that creates a web of interrelationships. Social novels tend to describe such a web; they fill their canvases with people so that we get a sense that we have a representative cross-section or sample of the country, or class of people, or subculture of the time. This canvas need not include everybody: in Dickens' and Balzac's novels it does—the rich and poor and middle class—but in Jane Austen's novel it includes primarily the upper middle class, in Updike's novel the middle class.

The creation of a social milieu is important because the main characters in social novels tend to define themselves through their contact with other people in society. Social inter-action—how people behave toward one another—is one of the crucial activities of the book. This is not to say that we do not have scenes of a character musing or brooding by himself. None-theless, much of what takes place in social novels is not inter-nalized within the individual; rather, it transpires in the open, between people. Thus Rabbit Angstrom, unhappy with his lot— a dull job, a loveless marriage, burdensome parenthood, and tedious social activities in his stifling little hometown—seeks to define his problems and solve them through confrontations with other people. Something is wrong with his life, and he thinks it would be corrected if he made his wife, Janice, understand him, if he could recapture the grace and glory of his old high school basketball days, if he had a love affair, if he got religion from his minister. So what takes place in *Rabbit, Run* is a series of human encounters. The encounters are usually as unproductive as this unpleasant little scene with Janice:

> He is indignant that she didn't see his crack about being a housewife. . . . There's no escaping it: she is dumb. . . .
> "Ah, Janice," he sighs, "Screw you. Just screw you."
> She looks at him clearly a long moment. "I'll get supper," she at last decides.
> He is all repentance. "I'll run over and get the car and bring the kid back. The poor kid must think he has no home. What the hell makes your mother think my mother has nothing better to do than take care of other people's kids?" Indignation rises in him again at her missing the point. . . .

Rabbit's assumption is that things will change. No society of people is static; their attitudes toward each other shift over the course of time. Each encounter with someone else produces a slight alteration in the interpersonal relationship, even if it is only a deepening of hostility or boredom. Rabbit goes to his former basketball coach to resuscitate the old relationship they had in school days, only to find that the coach has become a sot, and doesn't remember much of the old days. Rabbit's secret mo-ments with a new lover, Ruth, are equally frustrating in the long run, for they, too, simply drift into dullness. The social novel focuses on the dynamics of change, both between indi-viduals and within the larger economic and cultural organism (in this case the town of Brewer). We have, in such novels, a relatively sure sense of time passing and altering things. We are, in social novels, relatively well oriented as to what happens when and what follows what—how human relationships are built and ruined in the course of time. What has happened to

Rabbit's love for Janice? Why can't it be the way it used to be between him and his coach? Why can't he talk with his parents as he once did?

The depiction of experience unfolding through time constitutes a unique strength of the novel as a literary form. By its ability to transmit the sense of relationships changing, and by its emphasis on the sequential nature of human activities, the novel creates the illusion of the passage of time. It can cast us back into a character's childhood; it can guide us through the growth of a village, a society, a nation. Other literary forms do not lend themselves to such effects. The theater, for instance, must concentrate on a few scenes of revelation. Its audience would grow impatient if asked to sit through long reveries of childhood experience, or the gradual construction of a social world through a number of minor incidents involving secondary characters. The reader of the novel, on the other hand, expects his involvement with a book to be spread over a longer period of reading time, and he expects to be introduced to a world that may gradually take shape and change shape. Reading a novel is also a private experience, in which one moves at one's own pace, pausing at times to muse upon the book's creations, to daydream about the novel's people or action, to incorporate what one has read and thought about into one's own memory. The process of reading a novel induces the reader's imagination to spread out; the act of witnessing a stage play usually requires the spectator to focus his attention. The motion picture has the capacity to approach the novel's amplitude of scene and event, and to create a stronger sense than in the theater of the passing of time between one incident and another, but it, too, demands a commitment of its audience that rarely allows the imagination to spread as it does in the reading of fiction.

Given the capacity of the novel to create a sense of time passing and to induce its readers to expand imaginatively upon its material, it is only natural that fiction writers choose modes like the social novel (and, as we shall later see, the psychological novel) that can exploit those potentialities. Art forms presumably build upon the strengths of their own properties. Since there is room enough and time enough to portray numerous people, to depict whole societies, to extend our interests into the historical past, why not use the novel form to do so? Why not show man in his many social interactions? Why not attempt to capture the human dimensions of history and the dynamics of cultural and economic change? This, more than any other, is the reason why the social novel has been the dominant mode for 200 years.

Once we have identified a novel as being one in the social mode, how then should we go about interpreting it? What should we expect it to emphasize? One of the objectives, as we can all guess, is to acquaint us with the nature of the society that is depicted. We learn what life is like, what the shape of the society is, and what tensions exist within it. In *Rabbit, Run*, we perceive something of one level of American society. In a stunning, extended scene, in which Janice desperately tries to hold things together after Rabbit has left her, we discover how the confusion of responsibilities dominates ordinary lives.

> She drops to her knees, and the baby begins to cry. Panicked . . . she runs to the crib and nightmarishly finds it smeared with orange mess. "Damn you, damn you," she moans to Rebecca, and lifts the little filthy thing out and wonders where to carry her. . . . She takes the soaked daubed diaper to the bathroom and drops it in the toilet and dropping to her knees fumbles the bathtub plug into its hole. She pulls on both faucets as wide as they will go, knowing from experience that both opened wide make the right tepid mixture. . . . She notices the glass of whiskey she left on the top of the toilet and takes a long stale swallow. . . . [She sets Rebecca, the baby, on a living room chair.] She takes the crayons to the kitchen table and dumps the uneaten bacon and lettuce into the paper bag under the sink but the mouth of the bag leans partly closed and the lettuce falls behind into the darkness in back of the can and she crouches down with her head pounding to try to see it or get it with her fingers and is unable. . . . [She returns to the bathroom with Rebecca in her arms.] She is proud to be carrying this to completion; the baby will be clean. She drops gently to her knees by the big calm tub and does not expect her sleeves to be soaked. The water wraps around her forearms like two large hands; under her amazed eyes the pink baby sinks down like a gray stone.
>
> With a sob of protest she grapples for the child but the water pushes up at her hands, her bathrobe tends to float, and the slippery thing squirms in the sudden opacity. She has a hold, feels a heartbeat on her thumb, and then loses it, and the skin of the water leaps with pale refracted oblongs that she can't seize the solid of; it is only a moment, but a moment dragged out in a thicker time.
>
> [Finally pulling the baby out of the water, Janice tries to remember how to give artificial respiration.] . . . No spark kindles in the space between her arms; for all of her pouring prayers she doesn't feel the faintest tremor of an answer in the darkness against her . . . and she knows, knows, while knocks sound at the door, that the worst thing that has ever happened to any woman in the world has happened to her.

In these horrible, frantic moments leading to the accidental drowning of Rebecca, Janice has somehow been caught in what

Updike says is part of the texture of American life. The foolish obsession with cleanliness, the terrible responsibilities of wifehood and motherhood when one is not ready for them, the infuriating clutter of our lives—the bacon strips, the crayons, the garbage pails. It is a life of confusion, of hurry, of accident, of incompleteness. A day no different than many that Janice spends in terms of what she must do and how she handles it—except, of course, for the irreversible, horrible tragedy of it.

Janice's experience is horrible because we are too close to it. It is too similar to *our* experience. This is one of the objectives of a novel that creates a social situation in such depth and specificity: to draw us into the experiences vicariously. And thus when we encounter such a novel, we must understand that in interpreting it, we are being asked to interpret our own lives, for the fictional and the real are too close to avoid transferring meaning from one to the other. The fuller a novel's portrayal of society is, the more likely we are to feel as if we are part of it. The process of projecting ourselves into a lifelike fictional situation requires that we begin to respond to and evaluate that world in something of the way we do our own world. We make connections; we transfer meaning between fictional and real societies. Thus, when interpreting a social novel, we should expect to look for interpretations of the nature of the *society*—how it operates, what its dynamics are, what its values are—and we will often find ourselves discovering insights about human societies in general.

We can expect to look for patterns of human behavior, and often the crucial scenes between characters will be those which shape such patterns. While tracing patterns, we will find ourselves looking for the causes of things. In social novels, cause and effect seem much clearer and more explainable than in fiction of other modes, because we are observing the outward manifestations of human behavior, rather than the often inexplicable internal sources of motive. Janice Angstrom acts as she does because of Rabbit's treatment of her, and because of the numerous social pressures that we have seen working upon her. These are depicted through outward signs.

As one might expect, social novels frequently examine ethical questions. Since causes and effects are out there for us to see, and since the emphasis in such fiction is upon how human interrelationships form behavior, we can draw ethical conclusions more readily than in a novel where much of what transpires is internal—within the mind and sensibilities of the characters—or where it is symbolic. Hence, in interpreting novels in the social mode, we can anticipate that ethical issues will arise and be focused in a relatively objective form.

The death of Rabbit's and Janice's baby raises an ethical issue. Are they responsible for it, in some way? Is the death a hapless consequence of the mess they are making of their own lives? How do you assign *blame*? Rabbit can't bear the vague accusations of blame that he thinks are in everyone's mind, and he suddenly bursts out at the baby's burial:

> They misunderstand. He just wants this straight. He explains . . . "You all keep acting as if *I* did it. I wasn't anywhere near. *She's* the one." He turns to her, and in her face, slack as if slapped, sees that she too is a victim, that everyone is; the baby is gone, is all he's saying, he had a baby and his wife drowned it. "Hey it's O.K.," he tells her. "You didn't mean to." He tries to take her hand but she snatches it back like a trap and looks toward her parents, who step toward her.

Inchoately, Rabbit is trying to say that the cause lies back there in what we have seen of his life. It lies in those mixed up, loveless, frustrating human relationships, in the shape of life, the texture and values which make everything so difficult, so confusing, so petty, so slipshod. The answer to the ethical question can only be found in the web of relationships and the nature of American culture as Updike depicts it. *This* material is what we must understand and interpret in *Rabbit, Run*, ambiguous as that process will turn out to be.

The novel rose to prominence as a literary form at a time—the late eighteenth and early nineteenth centuries—when the reading public was confronted with these very kinds of questions: "How is the social order affecting individual behavior?" "What are the moral implications of life in an increasingly complex society?" They are age-old concerns, of course, but former religious and hierarchical social frameworks seemed to answer them better. By the eighteenth century, such frameworks were losing validity. In addition, people found themselves thrust into new and strange social milieus. The Industrial Revolution created a vastly larger middle class, and a new urban class. If one suddenly finds oneself in a new social station, as many people did, how does one act? Jane Austen's fictional dissection of upper middle-class manners helps answer the question. Stendhal's novels of young men from the country on the make in Paris furnish other perspectives on the case. Compounding the problem, of course, is the growth of the city—modern London and modern Paris—which presents situations unlike those of the former rural environments in which most people had lived. Daily routines, recreations, and work habits changed. The novel responded with Dickens' and Balzac's brilliant and exhaustive anatomies of the city life, or with retrospective, sometimes nostalgic pictures of the good old days in the country, from which somehow one could see how it all changed.

Change is the sensation of the nineteenth century. Change so fast and on such a scale that only a literary form like the social novel, with its ability to encompass many people and many events through time, could grasp it. Even the conception of history changed from that of preceding centuries. Wars now involved ordinary people and disrupted ordinary lives; earlier wars had been remote activities fought for obscure reasons by mercenary armies. The French and American revolutions, and the British parliamentary crises, brought people into the political process and made them factors in historical events. These were perfect circumstances for the novel that focuses on individuals acting in sociopolitical settings, and Sir Walter Scott took notice of this in creating the first best sellers of the novel. The novel was the ideal literary form for showing how society worked.

In summary, the realization that we are reading a novel that is primarily in the *social mode* poises us to ask the most appropriate and searching critical questions of it. For we can anticipate that the book will tell us something about the nature of society and therefore we should give those descriptions of the life of the times careful attention. We can assume that the texture of such life will figure into the crises of the individual characters, as it does in *Rabbit, Run*. We can expect that the issues will be shaped through human interrelationships, hence these deserve special study. We can anticipate that causes and effects will come forth relatively clearly and objectively. Finally, we can assume that ethical questions will arise more prominently in fiction of the social mode.

The value of working guidelines of this sort manifests itself when we turn to the mode of the psychological novel. Again, this is a term of convenience, for many of what I call social novels deal with the psychology of the characters—*Rabbit, Run* does, for instance. And psychological novels usually do give us pictures of society. But the psychological novel is organized according to the mental and emotional experience of one or a few characters, while the social novel is organized through social interaction. The focus of the psychological novel is on an individual's development: the movement of his thoughts, the forming of his personality and the complex internal motives that animate him. The term "psychological" does not mean, of course, that the character is psychoanalyzed, or even that everything is transmitted as if we were in the consciousness of the character (*how* a story is told will be the topic of Chapter 4). Rather, it means that the uniting principles of the novel—its focal areas—are the conflicts and developments taking place within one or a few characters.

How can we readily identify a novel in the psychological mode? First of all, much of the action in such a novel, as we might expect, is internal, transpiring as thoughts of the character. As an example, let me look at the "Quentin section" of William Faulkner's *The Sound and the Fury*. Faulkner's novel describes the agony of the Compson family, Old South aristocracy grown decadent. The book is presented in four sections, three of them refined through the consciousness of family members. Quentin Compson's section presents his thoughts on the day that he is to commit suicide, as he wanders about Cambridge, Massachusetts, and its environs, brooding upon his childhood, his incestuously tinged love for his sister Candace ("Caddy"), her marriage to a man he hates, the wreckage of his family life, and his alienation from his fellow students at Harvard, where he is attending college. There are some of what we would call events occurring during the day, but these events are important only as they relate to Quentin's own complex train of thoughts, as they trigger memory or cause his emotional wounds to fester. Similarly, we perceive the nature of a few places —we learn something about the Mississippi small town in which Quentin grew up, and we learn a little bit about Harvard—but what we learn more about is Quentin's mind and character. Action and sense of place, two tokens of the social novel, are sharply subordinated in the psychological mode. The organizing principle of Faulkner's material is the unfolding of Quentin's thought. Here is a typical paragraph:

> Why shouldn't you I want my boys to be more than friends yes Candace and Quentin more than friends *Father I have committed* what a pity you had no brother or sisters *No sister no sister had no sister* Dont ask Quentin he and Mr Compson both feel a little insulted when I am strong enough to come down to the table I am going on nerve now I'll pay for it after it's all over and you have taken my little daughter away from me *My little sister had no. If I could say Mother. Mother.*

Quentin is thinking back to a hated moment when his mother introduced him to Caddy's fiancé, a man Quentin detests.

Mother assumed her most vapid Old Southern gentility that evening, and babbled gratingly at the dinner table about how she wanted the two men, Quentin and Caddy's fiancé, "to be more than friends." This sets off the wry reflection that he and Caddy were "more than friends" and he recalls the confession he made to his father that he had "sinned" with his sister—a "sin" that he made up as a way of somehow trying to ostracize himself and Caddy from normal society. The recollection of his mother's behavior awakens old emotions, and Quentin bitterly reflects that his mother was never really a mother to him; he could not even bring himself to call her "mother": *"If I could say Mother. Mother."* Not all psychological novels present the individual's train of thought in quite such a dense and fragmented manner, but they do tend to focus, as this passage does, on the character's sensibility.

There are at least three moments in time contracted into the passage give above. One moment is that in which the thought occurs (the day in Cambridge). Another is that moment when Mother was suggesting at dinner that Quentin and Caddy's fiancé should be like brothers (this was in Mississippi some while back). A third is when he confessed to his father about his supposed sin with his sister. A further identifying characteristic of the psychological novel is that the sense of time is much more disorienting than in social novels. Material is not organized in the clear sequence found in social novels. Instead, the unfolding of the story is keyed to *psychologically significant moments* in the character's life. Sometimes that means that the narration will skip around from present to remote past to recent past. The movement is dictated in many instances by emotional impulses; an allusion, or an action, stimulates a buried or suppressed feeling that in turn leads us on to other times when that feeling arose. In any case, what is important are the formative moments in an individual's development or state of mind, moments that might not necessarily be socially significant. Indeed, they may have appeared trivial and inconsequential to the people involved, but intensely meaningful to the novel's protagonist. Accordingly, we will have difficulty making the same kind of objective situational judgments of human interaction that we could make in the social novel. In fact, one could say that the only important scene in Quentin's entire narration is the scene that we are witnessing as readers, in which Quentin thinks about his past and makes emotional connections out of all the fragments—the scene of Quentin *thinking.* Internally significant events, not externally significant ones, dominate the psychological novel.

The *aim* of the psychological novel is to enable us to understand the formation of feeling and attitude in the individual. We share his particular experiences. We apprehend the world in his uniquely personal manner. Quentin Compson's poignantly brief voyage through early twentieth-century American life is not like any other voyage. His is a case of guilt in search of a sin. His love for his sister is the sin that he conjures up, though he never commits the sinful act, and his suicide is to be the purging of it. There is nothing typical about Quentin Compson, though he shares the vague sense of guilt of those of his Southern heritage, and though he is in the agonies of self-doubt and self-hatred that many a young man experiences. The elements that have formed him are inimitable. Through Faulkner's novel we enter another man's consciousness and another track of experience that will never be duplicated, but that is human and enlarges our own sensibilities. Such, surely, is the objective of the psychological novel: to project us into the intensity of another individual experience. Quentin stares into the Charles River, to which he will soon commit himself:

> Where the shadow of the bridge fell I could see down for a long way, but not as far as the bottom. When you leave a leaf in water a long time after awhile the tissue will be gone and the delicate fibers waving slow as the motion of sleep. They dont touch one another, no matter how knotted up they once were, no matter how close they lay once to the bones. And maybe when He says Rise the eyes will come floating up too, out of the deep quiet and the sleep, to look on glory. And after awhile the flat irons would come floating up. I hid them under the end of the bridge and went back and leaned on the rail.

Only once in our experience—in Faulkner's novel—will we visualize that watery grave as Quentin does.

When reading a novel that has the indicia of the psychological mode, then, we should anticipate that our critical energies will be engaged not so much with understanding the nature and workings of society, or even how people interrelate, but how one individual experiences life. We will be looking for insights into a sensibility, and this, necessarily, is a highly subjective endeavor. No more than we can totally explain ourselves can we fully articulate the feel of another human sensibility when, as in fiction, we are given the opportunity to apprehend it. And so we will be looking less for objective data and more for those patterns and nuances of self-revelation that make up a man. Faulkner's creation of Quentin is composed of such nuances:

> I could feel water beyond the twilight, smell. When it bloomed in the spring and it rained the smell was everywhere you didnt notice it so much at other times but when it rained the smell began to come into the house at twilight either it would rain more at twilight or there was something in the light itself but it always smelled strongest then until I would lie in bed thinking when will it stop when will it stop. The draft in the door smelled of water, a damp steady breath. Sometimes I could put myself to sleep saying that over and over until after the honeysuckle got all mixed up in it the whole thing came to symbolise night and unrest I seemed to be lying neither asleep nor awake looking down a long corridor of grey halflight where all stable things had become shadowy paradoxical all I had done shadows all I had felt suffered taking visible form antic and perverse mocking without relevance. . . .

It is a marvelous thing to be able to be transported into another human experience as one is in art. In fiction we transcend the limitations of our individual state. In life we only know our inner experience and aspects of other people's outer behavior and demeanor. We have glimpses of their inner experience as they reveal it consciously or inadvertently. In fiction, however, we share extensively the inner experience of another individual.

Necessarily those issues that could be relatively sharply defined in the social novel will be more problematical in the psychological novel. Cause and effect will not be so clear-cut when we start to look inside people and discover the complex patterns of association, rationalization, and mood that underlie them. Similarly, we should not expect ethical issues to emerge in psychological novels as frequently or as unambiguously as in social novels. Quentin is wrapped up in guilt, but Faulkner is not asking us to judge him. Quentin's situation is so uniquely personal that it furnishes no guidelines for general behavior. That is simply not the concern of *The Sound and the Fury*. How, indeed, can we make assessments of the ethics of the way an individual thinks and feels? We can only and simply understand it. The novel is not asking us to do more. There are ethical implications in what we learn about other people; we can sympathize with them and figure out what moves them, and this can affect our judgments in real life situations. But the psychological novel generally does not require that we focus on moral judgments as an element in our interpretation.

The psychological novel veers away from social novels in another way. We noted that one indicator of the psychological mode was greater disorder in presentation. Time sense is disoriented, sequential relationships less in evidence. This suggests a diminished emphasis on *order* as a value in itself. Art, being selective, has a penchant for putting human experience in order. The social novel, with its grand overview, serves that purpose nicely. It flourished, as we noted, during the dramatic social and political upheavals of the nineteenth century because it could put that diversity and flux into ordered perspective and relationship. The psychological novel, on the other hand, may create a greater tolerance for disorder, or at least for the primacy of individual order. It reflects the Western yearning for personal freedom, and for the power to shape reality to one's own designs.

This factor may account in part for the turn in fiction writers toward the mode of the psychological novel in the second half of the nineteenth century. One must say, of course, that the novel has always been an art form of individualism. The Puritan emphasis on self-examination as a means of proving one's state of grace and one's spiritual worthiness influenced the rise to prominence of a literary form, the novel, which reflects the dynamics of that process. But the Puritan approach was largely to evaluate a man's life in terms of his social actions; outward behavior was an indicator of the inner state, moral rectitude the token of his uprightness. As the nineteenth century progressed the Puritan consciousness metamorphosed gradually within the ambiguities of modern experience and took on highly *personal* expressions. No longer was it correlated by objective, socially confirmed standards; instead it became more and more a matter of individual ethical consciousness. On the philosophical level, the religious world view of previous ages, in which it was assumed that activity on the human plane corresponded with divine designs, weakened its hold on the minds of men, and new philosophies of moral relativism arose. While it is true that such grand philosophical developments rarely affected writers directly in the nineteenth century, they had a way of insinuating themselves into modes of thinking. A novelistic form depicting that relativism—pointing out that the rights and wrongs of human behavior are difficult to sort out and evaluate, given the complexity and ambiguities of situations and the shading of motive and feeling in everyone—was destined to prove more adequate to the times. The psychological novel, as we have noted, captures those individual caprices and complications.

Finally, also, the inability of individual effort to affect societies as complex and disparate as modern industrial England and France—where economic and political power is distributed, and where governmental institutions have a propelling will of their own—defeats the power of any literary form to make coherent social readings. Dickens' heroic attempt to dominate and interpret all of his social world ended in frustration and despair. Balzac and Emile Zola in France exhausted their energies in futile efforts to map a world too big for any man's vision. Turn instead, argued Henry James and others of the late nineteenth century, to what is the only reality any individual can know: the experience of one's own consciousness.

The late nineteenth-century shift of emphasis toward the psychological novel corresponded with another development: the emergence of modern theories of psychology. Inevitably literature felt the impact of Freud's theories of the unconscious. A new dimension of human drama—the working out of anxieties in dreams, the psychic patterns of traumas and repressions, of wish fulfillments and sexual desires and death wishes—became available to the literary artist to explain human behavior. Psychologically informed philosophers like the American William James (Henry James' brother) and the Frenchman Henri Bergson suggested that human consciousness itself was a continually evolving process. Each person did not have a fixed personality, an established unchanging identity or nature, but was instead a consciousness that was in flux, changing, drifting, reacting, caught in its own inner stream of memories, sense impressions, highly personal images, tensions, and repressions. People were like Quentin Compson. They saw the world through unique lenses of consciousness, and thus, in a sense, they had their own reality. Why, then, try to create an objective reality in the novel, when everyone experiences it uniquely? Would it not be more realistic—that is, true to life—to dramatize individuals experiencing what is to them reality? Admittedly such fiction will have another shape, as it follows the individual consciousness, and it will look at different things, those things that are special to one or two individuals' experience, as in the psychological mode.

Thus, to recapitulate, we encounter in the novel of the psychological mode an emphasis on one person's experience at the cost of a grander picture of society. Conflicts are internal rather than out among other people; "action" is often within the mind rather than in the physical realm. We shall seek in such novels the apprehension of another individual's experience

—his way of thinking and perceiving things—rather than an insight into society's workings. We should pay attention to what the character thinks, what memories, aspirations, and anxieties gather together in him, so that we can understand how he sees things. We should be aware of the fact that every person and every thing in such a novel may be distorted to fit into his mood and perspective.

I observed a moment ago that the psychological novel tends to have a shape different from the social novel. We have discussed one aspect of that shape, a preoccupation with the experiences that are of importance to an individual, rather than with social and historical events. A further important change of shape occurs. If, as modern psychology tells us, the human personality is continually changing, then no social event is likely to be an end or climax to that change. Through much of the eighteenth and early nineteenth centuries, we were given novels that ended in marriage, or that reached a climax when the main character grew up or matured. Implicit in such novels is a concept of human nature: that a person becomes fixed, as it were, when he reaches the stability of adulthood (and a good marriage symbolized that stability). But if we believe, as many in the late nineteenth century did, that man keeps changing, isn't it arbitrary to end the story at this point, as if the characters' lives ended there? Consequently, by the last decades of the nineteenth century we get more novels that are open-ended. That is, they close at a point in the characters' lives that need not signify stability at all. We are given indications, in fact, that the characters will go on developing. In the novels of D. H. Lawrence and James Joyce, for instance, the main characters have reached no psychological resting point. They are as dissatisfied, restless, and ambitious at the close of the book as they were at the beginning of their experiences within the novel. We encounter more continued or renewed stories, in which characters reappear in subsequent novels. The novelistic forebears of the radio and television soap operas appear, in fact, as a kind of second-rate variation on this. The short story also comes into its own as a literary form in the late nineteenth century, for it is premised on continuing experience. The British writer E. M. Forster once described the short story as a "slice off the tapeworm of time."

There is another facet to this. Marriage, establishing a home, and landing a good position are social correlatives for happiness and fulfillment. They *represent* personal enrichment and success; they stand for it, in a way. But for later writers not only did marriage and landing a job seem to be merely way stations in the continuing drama of life, but no longer were they fulfilling ones. In the old days, when life was perhaps not changing as rapidly as it now was, marriage and a certain social position may really have been climaxes producing rewarding stability. For a great number of the late nineteenth-century novelists, however, social forms and social institutions were not what they were cracked up to be, and scarcely symbols of individual attainment. More and more novels ended with unsatisfactory marriages; we could hardly be convinced that the partners would live happily ever after. Or the life at the end of the book just never seemed to achieve its promise. This dissatisfaction with life, especially with middle-class life and its materialism, its unheroic everyday quality, contributed as well to the inclination to write fiction that did not devote itself to describing society and social institutions in lengthy detail. A nineteenth-century Frenchman, Gustave Flaubert, one of the most influential writers in the history of the novel, was so disgusted with the banal details of middle-class life that he said at times it made him physically ill. In *Madame Bovary*, he wrote a novel that portrayed the hopelessness and shallowness of that life and its social forms, especially marriage. As an aspect of this, he also argued against writing novels that devoted their energies to describing such a society and its unfulfilling and pointless interrelationships—that is, social novels.

Flaubert was driven by another purpose. He wanted to make the novel a better art form. Social novels by their nature mimic life, and life, we all know, is not very artistic. Social novels embraced congeries of events, delved into innumerable little nooks and crannies, chronicled dozens of lives, and spread themselves out over decades in an attempt to cover all the ground. They were, in the opinion of many writers, "great baggy monsters."

Flaubert, strongly supported by Henry James, instilled in writers the ideal of creating novels that were works of art, that were unified in artistic effect. Unnecessary actions or subplots that distracted from the principal action were to be avoided. Nothing extraneous or distracting should be included; all should work toward the expression of the meaning of the fictional experience described. An *imagery* should arise within the story that carries on the special associations that have gathered in our minds and in the minds of the characters around previous experiences. For, just as certain sights or sounds bring back associations in our mind with experiences in our pasts, we inevitably connect fictional characters with the images that occupy their thoughts or that recall something they once did. (We may, for

example, connect Quentin Compson with the image of him looking down into the Charles River, or with the sense picture he
created of night smells, the honeysuckle, etc.)

Novelists with such objectives are inevitably drawn to
poetry, and early in the twentieth century a number of important writers—James Joyce, Marcel Proust, André Gide—developed a fascination with the artistic possibilities suggested by the
nineteenth-century French poetic movement called symbolism.
The symbolists wrote poems that concentrated on private, individual experiences—experiences so unusual that they could be
communicated only through special metaphors. Each poem expressed something that perhaps only the poet had felt in that
particular way, and the sensation could be transmitted only
through those images and associations clustered around it. The
poet sought to induce his reader to experience something of the
same sensation—to see and feel the moment as he did.

It seemed an inevitable step from the psychological novel,
which emphasized individual experience, to a novel that attempted to transmit a unique impression or sensation. Similarly
the urge in Flaubert's successors to create a novel with greater
artistic balance and intensity led them to a fiction conceived
after symbolist poetry. Rather than pursue the convoluted mean-
derings of an individual sensibility through its disparate experiences of growth and maturity, through its various states and
dispositions, why not concentrate on a single state of mind,
single emotions, or perhaps a cluster of feelings and ideas?
Such a scheme would lend itself to deeper intensity, sharper focus, greater artistic integration. All the experiences and all the
images in the novel would relate to or illustrate the governing
state of mind or feeling that the novel explores. The book would
itself unfold into a kind of extended image. And like the symbolist poem, the novel would induce the reader to experience
those special sensations that characterize the state of mind or
feelings.

Thus *The Lime Twig*, a novel by the contemporary American novelist John Hawkes, explores and elaborates upon unique
sensations and experiences that relate to modern man's sense of
impotence and insufficiency. The characters in the novel all
seem to be bound into this human concern: men who fail in
love, who are weakened by conflicting emotions toward mothers
or wives, who feel powerless, or who can impose themselves on
others only through desperate acts of brutality. The novel im-
presses the reader with images that evoke this particular condition. One image is of a crippled bomber (also a symbol of

disabled masculinity) suspended as if enchanted over London during the blitz, connoting the impotence we feel in modern life when war and suffering are visited upon us. Another image is of a larger-than-life, statuesque horse (the classic symbol of male virility) emerging out of the darkness, and mocking the men in the novel. And the episodes—beatings by gangsters, orgies—are all correlated with the governing human situation of the book. It is as if a *state of being* were explored in various complex, impressionistic ways. The language of the novel, dramatic, highly charged, and ironic, intensifies the reader's involvement in the state of being. All aspects of the art contribute to vivifying the specific nature of the human experience.

We have worked our way to the third mode, the *novel of symbolic action*. To a certain extent the novel of symbolic action can be identified by its difference from the other two modes. For we see neither a detailed description of a recognizable society in all its variety, nor an extended in-depth psychological portrait of a character. In fact, the social setting often appears to be deliberately unreal, isolated, or bizarrely exaggerated. And the characters are in states of remarkable intensity, and lacking in the sort of complex motives and varied patterns of thought that constitute full, individualized characterization.

Anthony Burgess' *A Clockwork Orange* illustrates the novel of symbolic action. It is narrated by a teenaged tough named Alex, who is leader of a street gang in a London that is projected a few years in the future, but that bears unsettling resemblance to the contemporary scene. For Alex and his gang, the only entertainment is beating up people they meet on the streets at night. They come upon an old man carrying books from the library. They surround him and then taunt him. One of the boys grabs a book on elementary crystallography and insists that it's a dirty book. "You're nothing but a filthy-minded old skitebird," he smirks, "You deserve to be taught a lesson." He rips the pages of the book out and scatters them on the street. Then the boys start to work on the old man himself. The novel is narrated in a street slang, but the violence is not lost:

> Pete held his rookers [arms] and Georgie sort of hooked his
> rot [mouth] wide open for him and Dim yanked out his false
> zoobies [teeth], upper and lower. He threw these down on the
> pavement and then I treated them to the old bootcrush. . . . The
> old veck began to make sort of chumbling shooms—'wuf
> vaf wof'—so Georgie let go holding his goobers [lips] apart and
> just let him have one in the toothless rot with his ringy fist,
> and that made the old veck start moaning a lot then, then out
> comes the [blood], my brothers, real beautiful. . . .

"Real beautiful" the sight of blood is to Alex; indeed we soon discover, as gang fights, rapes, tortures, terrorization, and other brutality unfold, that Alex achieves a certain aesthetic pleasure from violence. It's his art form. The only other pleasure in his life is a love for classical music, but that love is connected with brutality, for Beethoven and Bach stir him to greater ecstasies of random hatred. A curious connection, that, for it could mean that violence really does have its aesthetic, or that music is simply a form of expression that is also potentially violent. *A Clockwork Orange* is about evil and it is about self-expression. For, offended as we are with Alex's callousness, we find ourselves reading on with fascination. Why are most of us so compelled by descriptions of evil? Why are the villains so interesting; why does terrifying action whet our interest? Curious and disturbing changes take place in us during the reading process. We ourselves become more callous to the horrors of the story. (Indeed, this was one of the objections to the movie version of *A Clockwork Orange*: that films of this sort may make audiences insensitive to brutality.) We even grow to like Alex. For Alex turns out to be the only vital human being in the jaded, heavily socialistic society of *A Clockwork Orange*. All the adults, including Alex's parents, lead plodding lives doing dull work and watching the telly. The government officials who finally catch up with Alex are equally brutal but lack his style and verve, or they are grey, venal bureaucrats who are willing to brainwash him in the name of social peace.

Emerging here is the identifying characteristic of the novel of symbolic action. It is a novel written primarily *to dramatize a theme*. *A Clockwork Orange* is built around a theme—that of violence as human expression. The aesthetic pleasure of brutality may be more properly defined as a state of mind, but Burgess does, as we shall see, enlarge it into a philosophical concern.

When we encounter a twentieth-century novel (for the novel of symbolic action is essentially a twentieth-century phenomenon, growing out of the evolution in thinking about the novel form that I described above), we can assume that our critical task is to understand its theme. Admittedly Burgess may be warning us that English and American society is on the way to the *Clockwork Orange* model, but his book can hardly be considered a realistic anatomy of a recognizable society as, say, Updike's is. Too much is missing from the social picture; the texture of ordinary lives has been omitted. If anything, this is an exaggeration of one aspect of a society, isolated from normal contexts, blown up to nightmarish proportions. The mode of the novel of symbolic action almost always has that identifying characteristic of distorted but graphically strong focus.

Alex has parents, but we rarely see them. He presumably had a childhood, but we are told nothing about it. He is very *real*, but he has no complexity of emotions, no shifts of thought, as Quentin does, to other times and other places. He has one besetting obsession, and that is all we know about him. Characters in novels of symbolic action are often like that: shown only in the grip of the governing state of being. Often they are two-dimensional, even at times comic strip types. For the objective of the novel is to transmit the state of being and the ideas concerning it. Thus it is misleading to criticize a book of this sort for having uncomplex characters. This is an error into which many critics of the contemporary novel have fallen.

The other characters in novels of symbolic action tend to be even less fully developed. They are placed in the book so that facets of the themes may be reflected by their behavior. Thus, in *A Clockwork Orange*, when Alex is finally arrested for his career of crime, he is subjected to brainwashing in an attempt to cure him of violent tendencies. The men who program him are faceless administrators of the bureaucratic society, and even the most individually delineated of them, the prison chaplain, exists only to expound on the idea that is at stake here. Alex's reform is accomplished by strapping him to a chair, taping his eyelids open, then compelling him to watch films of torture and human dismemberment while under the influence of a drug that sickens him whenever he sees blood. Gradually Alex develops a physical reflex against violence. His mind is as vicious as ever, but the first movement toward physical assault makes him retch. The prison chaplain fights against Alex's treatment on the grounds that it is not reform at all, for Alex has made no decision to be good. The chaplain argues that Alex avoids violence not for moral reasons, but for uncontrollable physical ones. " 'Goodness comes from within,' " the chaplain contends, " 'Goodness is something chosen. When a man cannot choose he ceases to be a man.' " Burgess' focus on the human potentiality for evil, on the almost aesthetic pleasure that comes from it, and upon our fascination with its perverse vitality, confronts the reader with the issue whether evil is not something natural to the human condition. If a society programs its members out of the ability to make a choice, can their good acts be truly called good? Burgess' issue has substantial religious implications, for the ability to will goodness implies also its opposite: the ability to perform evil. *A Clockwork Orange*, by thrusting us into the dramatic context through our empathy with Alex and our revulsion/fascination over the novel's events, presents that problem in the immediacy and ambiguity of human response that is, as I have maintained, the unique power of fiction to elicit.

We must be wary not only of expecting too much of characters in novels of symbolic action, but also of reading the action in the book too literally. After Alex is "cured," for instance, he is released from prison and goes back into society. He then has a series of encounters with the victims of his previous brutality. Since violence now nauseates him, he cannot defend himself, and one of the first people he meets is the old man whose books he helped tear up and whose false teeth he stomped on. It is in the library, and the old man and his decrepit companions set upon Alex "with their feeble rookers and horny old claws," screaming and beating on him for all they are worth. This encounter and similar ones with his other victims from the old days have too much poetic justice to claim lifelikeness. They are symbolic actions. In fact, because Alex is going through a very powerful self-destructive phase at the time, they may very well be projections of his desire for punishment. The world of the novel at this point is the world of his state of mind; what occurs here is a reflection of his mood, his way of looking at himself and everything around him. Action in novels of this mode is often *symbolic*, as the name of the mode suggests, and intended as a dramatization of the book's *ideas, mood,* or *state of mind,* rather than a literal translation of reality.

In approaching the novel of symbolic action for the purposes of criticism, we should recognize—by the isolated, intensified, often hallucinatory focus of its action, and the limited insight we are given into the characters' full development—that it is an idea we must look for. Sometimes that idea is philosophical, sometimes it is an idea about human nature. In the latter instance, the novel may be darkened or bent—or brightened to horrible clarity—by a governing emotional situation. The world will be sensed through a mood; everything in it will be projected like imaginary figures on a wall. The underlying tension may be the anxiety of that emotion, felt ultimately in ourselves as we participate in symbolic activity (as will be illustrated in the next chapter).

The novel since the beginning of the twentieth century has employed the mode of symbolic action because it seems to suit the times. In support of those pressures within literary tradition—the desire to make the novel more artistic, the impact of symbolist poetry, the fascination with a highly unique personal perspective—there have been social and philosophical developments converging toward such expression. The belief that each of us sees reality through our own distorted lens of sensibility has been reinforced by new scientific findings about the nature of human perception. There is evidence to say that we literally see only what we have been psychologically prepared to see. At the same time, the century's greater interest in abnormal psychology attunes us to visions of reality that are strangely intense. The concept of human existence called the absurd, which argues that life has no sensible pattern or any imperative for a specific set of ethics or ideals, finds its natural expression in a bizarre fictional context of illogical sequence and absurd characterization. Modern history, with its Auschwitz, its hydrogen bomb, its Disneylands, could call for no other artistic expression. Finally, there has been an explosion of ideas in the twentieth century unequalled in any previous period of equal duration, and the novel has been a dramatic testing ground for these ideas.

The novel of symbolic action resembles in certain respects an eighteenth and nineteenth-century narrative mode, that of the *modern romance*. Many novels of symbolic action have been fertilized by the same vision as the romance, but there are substantial enough differences in outlook to consider the modes separately.

I use the term *modern romance* to distinguish it from the classic romance, such as the old Greek love idyll *Daphnis and Chloe* (you surely are familiar with *Daphnis and Chloe*), because ancient romances dealt with idealized characters and situations, often mythical figures—gods and goddesses—in a traditional story, a cultural mythos. The modern romance is hardly idealized, and its story, though often strange and unnatural in many respects, is original not traditional, and is grounded in the reality of the time. The best known of the modern romances, Emily Bronte's *Wuthering Heights*, will define the mode for us.

We enter a special world in the modern romance. The settings are frequently isolated—in the back reaches where civilization has barely penetrated, in remote forests, rural areas, or highland wilds where men seem to be living out primitive emotions. *Wuthering Heights* takes place in the moors of northeast England, within a dark and brooding house that is a rabbit warren of hidden rooms, closets, and staircases. The story is told by a city man, Lockwood, whose nerve-wracking encounter with the violent, petulant Heathcliff, the dark savage man who dominates the mansion, has led him to ask an old housekeeper, Nelly Dean, to recount the uncanny tale of the novel. Neither Lockwood nor Nelly Dean is likely to be a totally truthful story-teller, and much of what Nelly narrates is scarcely believable. The facts are obscure, as if seen through mist. These traits iden-tify the modern romance: events occurring in isolation, away from ordinary social environments, are related to us indirectly, handed down verbally, with the reliability of the account in question because it is all so strange and wondrous. In keeping with this, our sense of time in romances is curiously suspended. The sequence of events—what happened after what—is reason-ably clear, but unimportant. Time is not measured by the normal standards of social activities and human development. History, in the public sense, is ignored. Years are telescoped, yet mo-ments are extended. The people appear to live outside the refer-ence of chronological time. Heathcliff, and his "sister"/lover, Catherine, seek to retain in adulthood the intense relationship of their childhood. When Catherine dies, largely by her own will because the force of Heathcliff's feeling for her—and hers for him—is too intense to permit their existence together, Heath-cliff vows to join her in death. And although years pass before he dies, they are as one moment of agony for him. There is also the uncanny legend that Catherine's body does not decay in her grave until Heathcliff joins her. Emotions are frozen, develop-ment is only a festering of pain: "time stagnates here."

The characters in the modern romance loom larger than life, or more intense than any of us could be. Heathcliff is su-perhuman in his energy, and occasionally in his savagery. He is gripped by demonic force. In order to spite Catherine, he marries another, an "ordinary" young woman, hangs his new wife's pet dog, and devotes himself to driving her to insanity and death because she is too feeble and unspirited for him. It takes Heath-cliff years to destroy himself, because his constitution is so strong that it withstands immensities of activity, suffering, and self-punishment. His and Catherine's love is described as the most powerful in mankind. "If all else perished," Catherine says, "and Heathcliff remained, I should still continue to be. My love for Heathcliff resembles the eternal rocks beneath. . . . I *am* Heathcliff." Ordinary humans, with their ordinary emotions, pale before these two. Catherine and Heathcliff burn into our imaginations as do few other creations in literature. It is almost as if they came out of another dimension—out of legend, or myth, or recesses in our psyche long suppressed by civilization.

The action in a modern romance, therefore, often remains unexplained. Motivations do not grow out of response to the circumstances, as they do in social novels; attitudes spring full blown into the consciousness. So powerful are they that a deep psychological tension seems to have been unleashed, but we are given none of the insight into sensibility and individual evolution that inheres in the psychological novel. People confront each other in the modern romance, as they might in the social novel, but they rarely interact. Interhuman relations appear to be dramatizations of the forces within. The discriminations that emerge from social and psychological novels—showing how ambiguous all questions of ethics are, or how much of what all of us do is a compound of weakness and willfulness and chance —are played down in the modern romance.

Not all characters in the modern romance have quite such godlike dimensions as Catherine and Heathcliff, but all are gripped with such intensity. The focus is different from that in the twentieth-century novel of symbolic action, however, for the romance's attention is not limited to a single state of being or to a central idea. The modern romance is a perspective on tensions within its contemporary social order; it is an abstracted vision of the *state of human society* in its larger forms, not a focus on one problem or one kind of human experience within that society.

Wuthering Heights, for instance, appeared in 1847, the heyday of the English social novel, and stood as an uncanny, difficult-to-categorize contrast to the picture those novels drew of the times. Remote and specialized as *Wuthering Heights'* fictive world seemed to be, it nonetheless dealt with the tensions that underlay the Victorian social world. Nineteenth-century England, in the process of the dizzying social and economic change that I spoke of, was worried about the breakdown of order. Heathcliff symbolizes that breakdown. His household is chaos: starving, snarling dogs prowl; blood hatreds break out; a queer, preachy old man lurks in the back stairway. Heathcliff is a tyrant, imprisoning a young girl and making his son into an illiterate ungainly animal. *Wuthering Heights* dramatizes much of what is being suppressed in ordinary Victorian society. The awesome energy of Heathcliff also corresponds to the sense of uncontrollable energy fulminating in the England of the times, when steam power was leashed, the railroads created, and men acted as political masses.

The love of Catherine and Heathcliff contrasts with the refined and seemingly diminished love stories of the English social novel. It suggests that a valuable intensity in our human relationships has been lost in our civilizing process. But the self-destructiveness of the love in both of them indicates that perhaps love so powerful and absorbing could not be endurable in human cultures. *Wuthering Heights*, in these and other ways, reflects upon its times in a complex manner. Modern romances, such as Bronte's book and Hawthorne's *A Scarlet Letter*, emerge in modern societies in order to remind the culture of what lies beneath it. They expose the tensions that are covered up by the veneer of manners and our everyday lesser preoccupations. They isolate for intense dramatization the fears, the desires, the conflicts that exist in muted form among us. Sometimes, as in *Wuthering Heights*, sexual taboos like incest, which it would have been unthinkable to treat in ordinary situations with ordinary people, are tapped. In our critical study of such books, it is helpful to know that these tensions and yearnings are what we must interpret. Not the sensibilities of the characters, for they are stylized creations, larger than life, opaque as to their motivations and development. Not the social fabric, for modern romances are set in isolated or fringe areas, with much of the everyday pattern of life blocked out. Not the ethics of the situation, for people in romances seem to be urged on by considerations that do not arise in social interaction. Not the governing state of being (as in novels of symbolic action), for modern romances have a broader reach into the foundations of human behavior, into mythic and archetypal human patterns, and they are acted out in a more extended way. They are not designed to analyze an idea or state of being; often, indeed, what inspires the romance is obscure even to the author.

The modern romance is a relatively rare creature among novels—so rare that you almost instinctively know when you are in its atmosphere. It is significant, however, not only for what it tells us about our more civilized social and psychological novels, but also because it exposes the bare structure of story, and of emotion in response to story, that is so instrumental in our reading experience. To that structure we now must go.

Structure and Plot:
Fairy tale desires · Lost expectations · Paranoia

> "'Hold your noise!' cried a terrible voice, as a man started up
> from among the graves at the side of the church porch. 'Keep
> still, you little devil, or I'll cut your throat!'
>
> "A fearful man, all in coarse grey, with a great iron on his
> leg. A man who had been soaked in water, and smothered
> in mud, and lamed by stones, and cut by flints, and stung by
> nettles, and torn by briars; who limped, and shivered, and
> glared, and growled; and whose teeth chattered in his head,
> as he seized me by the chin.
>
> "'Oh! Don't cut my throat, sir,' I pleaded in terror. 'Pray
> don't do it, sir.'"

THIS is the first incident of Charles Dickens' novel *Great Expectations*. The narrator, Pip, is describing one of the early vivid events of his childhood; he is seized, when alone in the marshes, by an escaped criminal, Magwitch, and told to expect all kinds of horrible tortures if he does not steal some food for the criminal. It is a good beginning for any book because we are immediately drawn into a tense, dangerous situation and we are in suspense over the outcome. It gives us a good opportunity also to discover how novels are structured, how our interests and our own projections about what will happen are manipulated, how *plot* operates, and to see how we are guided toward the meaning of the experiences in the novel.

Right away, you recall, we could reasonably estimate what *Henderson the Rain King* was going to be about. This is not the case with Dickens' novel, but we are likely to read on for two reasons. First out of curiosity to learn what will happen to Pip. An opening scene in which a desperate convict terrorizes a little boy promises more excitement. The love of a good story, of fast moving, emotionally charged events is what attracts us to many books. It is what makes night-time addicts of mystery novel readers; it is what saved Scheherazade's head for 1001 nights.

The second reason why Dickens is likely to hold onto us is more important and elusive. The terror of Pip reminds us oddly and vaguely of our own childhood nightmares of being kidnapped or menaced. The "bogeyman" probably still haunts many of our psyches. The first stories that caught our imaginations, in fact, may have been the legends or rumors that children hear, or forbidden stories, or shows of mystery or violence. Classic fairy tales often dwell on childhood fears. Hence we come to *Great Expectations*—and Dickens knew this—with our own story situations from childhood. We know all too well Pip's fright.

Our picture of childhood terror becomes stronger with the next blood-curdling threat from Magwitch:

> " 'There's a young man hid with me, in comparison with which young man I am a angel. That young man hears the words I speak. That young man has a secret way pecooliar to himself of getting a boy, and at his heart, and at his liver. It is in wain for a boy to attempt to hide himself from that young man. A boy may lock his door, may be warm in bed, may tuck himself up, may draw the clothes over his head, may think himself comfortable and safe, but that young man will softly creep and creep his way to him and tear him open.' "

The predicament that Pip finds himself in seems to promise for us a novel of mysterious and disturbing events. It indicates to us, also, *a vision of a world*: a world in which people appear out of mists and darkness, in which a boy can be hounded to the end of his days by men desperate enough to tear his heart and liver out. Dickens projects a murky, probably evil world, tainted with criminality and fear. (Later, as events unfold, our initial impression will be reinforced, for Dickens envisioned nineteenth-century England as a dark and corrupted society.)

Other novels give us radically different worlds. Jane Austen's *Pride and Prejudice* and *Emma* open in the drawing rooms of comfortable, well-lighted houses where people are talking in a lively way. Her books are not haunted by evils and apprehensions as Dickens' novel is. Ernest Hemingway's *The Sun Also Rises* immediately sets out, as we will discuss in Chapter 7, a world of empty activity, irritated people, and boredom. Some of Anthony Trollope's nineteenth-century novels begin with arguments about politics and social change among relatively well-established people. From our sense of the kind of world that the novelist is creating, we can usually predict the kinds of events that will fill the novel: domestic problems in the case of *Emma*; political confrontations in the case of a Trollope novel; criminality and mysterious interference with other people in *Great Expectations*. I suspect that almost all of us make these kinds of predictions about a novel's world; how often have we stopped reading a book shortly after we got into it with the observation that "this is not the kind of thing I am interested in reading about"?

This, then, is the *first* of the three principal elements that form the structure of a novel and that determine the novel's meaning: *our expectations about the nature of the novel's world*. It is the element that first grips us in most books, and yet it is the one least accounted for in analyzing the structure of a book. This is surprising because one of the elements that differentiates the novel from poetry and drama is that the novel establishes its own world.

Our expectations about the world of *Great Expectations*, as a matter of fact, are the only projections that we can confidently make about the novel from the first few chapters. Though we know that Pip is recounting his childhood adventures, we do not know whether the book will devote itself entirely to childhood experiences, or whether it will trace Pip's development from child to adult. Even the emphasis he places upon the sense of guilt and unworthiness he was made to feel—which might suggest that the novel will describe how Pip "went bad" and was punished for it, or reformed—does not firmly establish a pattern for the book that will enable us to predict generally the direction it will take.

Such speculations about the direction and scope of the book are more common to our reading process than we may think. Readers are always trying to orient themselves in the strange world of a new novel, and this means that projections are constantly being made about the shape of the story. We do not necessarily try to predict what specific events will occur, but rather how far in the character's life it will take us, what range of experiences will be involved, what the goals of the character appear to be, what are likely to be the fates of the characters.

Some readers are so impatient to know what will happen in a novel that they peek ahead to the last chapter. Anxiety of that sort is caused by our identification with the characters. By sharing some sense of Pip's awe and fright, by placing ourselves imaginatively in the predicament of any fictional character who is living out fears or worries or joys that we have at some time experienced or thought of ourselves, we establish the involvement with character and situation that is necessary to plot. The more psychologically committed we are to the people in a novel, the more likely we will begin to think ahead to what might happen to them. As our interest in character increases, we try to anticipate the future turn of events—even what the likely outcome of the story will be. Consequently, we begin to interact with the author, setting up our desired or expected plot against the one we are following.

The first chapters of *Great Expectations*, as with many books, are given over, in large part, to extending and deepening our identification with, and sympathy for, Pip. We learn not only of his frights, but of his aspirations to be free of his overbearing grown sister, who reluctantly took over responsibility for him after his parents died, and who mercilessly cuffs and bullies him. We come to appreciate the fondness that he feels for his sister's husband, Joe, who tries awkwardly to protect the boy. Hence we gradually develop our own conception of what we would like to see happen to Pip in the novel. In addition, we see more and more clearly that the novel is very likely to concern Pip's efforts to be independent and free of the fears and oppressions that dominate his childhood. That is, after all, what Dickens has interested us in, and if we were to make a guess about the outlines of the book (based on other, similar books we have read), that is what we would predict. We are formulating the *second* of the three principal elements that dictate the structure of a novel and that determine the novel's meaning; *our concern over what will happen to the characters, and the expectations that we have about what will happen to them.*

The first promising indication of the scope of *Great Expectations*, of what aspects of Pip's life the novel will cover, and what he is struggling toward, comes when Pip is sent to play at the house of a reputedly wealthy and eccentric old woman, Miss Havisham. The house has been barricaded against outsiders for years, and Miss Havisham is ghoulishly wasted away, living among spiders and mice and decayed shreds of her past. She lives in this seclusion with a beautiful golden-haired girl named Estella, who has nothing but contempt for her new playmate

Pip—" 'Why, he is a common labouring boy!' "—and who is told by Miss Havisham to break Pip's heart. These are surely the elements of a fairy tale: a poor but ambitious boy, a beautiful princess who is above his station in life, and a wicked old crone who has kept the princess a virtual prisoner and wants to see the boy suffer. It would be impossible for any reader not to project a likely pattern for this story: Pip will grow up to be rich and handsome; he will earn the love of the beautiful Estella; and he will free her from the cruel influences of Miss Havisham. And, of course, they will live happily ever after. If the novel follows the lines of this classic fairy-tale sequence, we can anticipate its general plot very clearly.

Certainly we have a better notion now of the potential reach of the novel's events: it will follow Pip's story into adulthood and, apparently, will describe his efforts not only to become independent, but to acquire a fortune and prove worthy of Estella, probably by overcoming any obstacles to their marriage and by dispelling the evil that so haunts his life. If you say that this seems too fanciful a plot for anyone to spin for himself while he is reading a novel, I would remind you how often you have, in the course of reading, expected that the basic plot would be a love story, or that a particular character would be murdered. We are full of more potential plots than we recognize, and Dickens would not have established so patent a fairy-tale situation unless he expected that we would pick it up and fill out its pattern.

The problem here, however, is that fairy tales rarely come true and they rarely resemble actual life. Pip had appealed to us because he seemed so human, so similar to us that we could identify with him. If he is to live the life of a fairy-tale hero, the novel will lose its close relationship to our experience. So we cannot help but be uneasy about the unrealistic plot pattern that Dickens now seems to have put upon the characters and events of the book.

The contrast between the fairy-tale pattern and that which we would expect from a realistic story of growing up is heightened by the ensuing episodes in Pip's life, which take him into London, where he tries to come to terms with existence in the competitive, indifferent city. There is even here an unrealistic element in Pip's experiences as a young man out in the world, for he is being financed by an unknown benefactor who wants him to learn to be a "gentleman," but he is nonetheless far from the idealized hero of fairy tales. He goes through the same traumas over leaving home and giving up old friends, and the same confusions and indecision, that most of us experience. Had the fairy-tale situation not been introduced, we would predict that *Great Expectations* would be a novel about attaining adulthood —coming to terms with the real world. And that, as we all know, is a complex enough process. It means—depending on your scale of values—attaining emotional or financial independence, understanding oneself better, acquiring the ability to formulate one's own moral principles, discovering the right kind of occupation or cause, becoming a "success," or achieving happiness— a vast number of possible goals, not all of them mutually consistent.

Here it is important to make a distinction between the bases of our projections about the experiences of a character in a novel. If *Great Expectations* had none of the fairy-tale elements, we would rely on our own real life experiences in growing up (and perhaps on some books that we had previously read that dealt realistically with the process of becoming an adult), and on what we know about Pip's personality and character, to predict what he would go through. These estimates of the rough outlines of the novel are essentially derived, as you can see, from real life and from our acquaintance with realistic characters. It is these projected patterns, these expectations of what will happen to the character, that I had in mind when I suggested the second principal element that determines the novel's structure: our concern for the characters as fellow humans and our expectations about what will happen to them.

The fairy-tale pattern in *Great Expectations* is not one that grows out of our real life experience, however, or even out of our understanding of Pip's personality. It is a pattern that has been imposed on the situation by Dickens. It is an artificial structuring of human experience that comes out of storytelling and the literary tradition, and its appeal is not that it describes our real experience, but that it sets out, in a simplified and exaggerated way, our wishes and anxieties. This kind of structure I would set apart as the *third* principal element that determines the structure of a novel and its meaning: *expectations dictated by traditional plot or story formulas*. Sometimes this element is not in a novel at all; sometimes it so dominates a novel that we feel that the characters have no human life on their own—that they are tools of an artificial plot. Sometimes, as in *Great Expectations*, these formulas are contrasted with realistic experience. Dickens' own rapid rise to fame and fortune had seemed like a fairy tale to him; as he grew older, however, the problems of real life seemed to make a cruel joke out of life as a "fairy tale come true," and he often contrasted the two. The consequence of this will become clearer as we go on.

It is useful to pause periodically in the reading of a novel and ask ourselves: "Where, at this point, is the novel heading?" "What do I think, in general terms, is the likely plot?" "What do I want to see happen to the characters?" We ask these questions unconsciously as we read along, for it is part of human character to try to figure out what a book is about in order not to be lost or confused as we read on. Indeed, most writers work on the assumption that readers are trying to figure out what will happen next and are building up interest in the characters (hoping the admirable characters will "come to a happy ending," and the despicable characters will "get what they deserve"), and it is by guiding and revising those expectations and desires that the writer affects the reader.

When we are aware of the nature of our expectations about the events that are to come, we can see how the author is modifying them, maneuvering us toward specific attitudes. For instance, about midway through the book we discover that Pip can only realize his own "great expectations" of becoming a gentleman by betraying his old friend and protector, Joe. When Joe visits Pip in London, Pip is embarrassed to see him and ashamed to introduce him to his new city acquaintances. He is especially afraid to let Joe be seen by Bentley Drummle, the man Pip most detests in the world, and he reflects that "throughout life our worst weaknesses and meannesses are usually committed for the sake of the people whom we most despise." Pip discovers that the London he so much desired is a place of viciousness, coldness, and cutthroat dealings. In a sequence of episodes, we observe that wretchedness and suspicion are the inhuman conditions of the modern city. The best that anyone can hope for is to live a divided life like Pip's city friend Wemmick who has two personalities: one for work which is so rigid and unfeeling that his mouth resembles a mailbox slot, and the other for home where he is cheery, kind, and relaxed. It is through scenes involving secondary characters (as we will discuss further in Chapter 6) that our outlook on Pip's situation changes. When a writer is skillful, and interprets our responses correctly, the events and changing relationships in the novel can shift our desires for the characters. Slowly but surely, the success we anticipated for Pip —becoming a gentleman of wealth and leisure—no longer looks as attractive as it once did. We are inclined to think, as we read on, that maybe Pip would be better off if he were poorer but happier, and more decent to his old friends. We modify *our* definition of what we desire for Pip—not independence and worldly success, but rather the fulfillment and humaneness that consideration for other people brings. By maneuvering us into changing the nature of what we wish for Pip, Dickens steers us toward accepting a new range of values, the values that *he* thinks are most important. The significance of Pip's experience is coming clear.

In the meantime, we grow disillusioned with the rewards that the fairy tale promises. Estella proves to be an ice-cold princess: her warped upbringing has prevented her from developing any human warmth and she is incapable of love. Every effort that Pip makes to ingratiate himself with Estella is demeaning to him and a sacrifice of his old moral principles. Dickens demonstrates not only that fairy tales do not come true, but that an attempt to live as if they did weakens one's will to act independently, for the dangerous allure of such fantasies is that good things magically happen to people without their making positive efforts in their own behalf. We can see now that the fairy-tale formula in the novel does not work against those expectations and desires that we built up out of our identification with Pip as a lifelike character engaged in realistic experiences. On the contrary, the defeat of the expectations dictated by the fairy-tale formula reinforces our conviction that humane qualities bring the most genuine satisfactions and that they require positive individual effort.

Finally, even the underlying source of anxiety that Dickens' vision of the world inspires is developed toward the close of the novel in such a way that it amplifies the meaning of Pip's experience. You recall that from the opening scene in which Magwitch appears out of the mists we sense that the world of *Great Expectations* is one of criminality and corruption, in which men connive to sink their hooks into other men. This vision is intensified throughout the novel, as a complicated network of insidious interrelationships among the characters is established. Magwitch, still a desperate fugitive, reenters Pip's life and we feel the same dread and disgust that Pip does. Our anxieties for a character can structure a novel in much the same way that our positive desires can. Yet as events unfold we learn that Magwitch has been victimized by a venal society and our attitude toward him changes as Pip's does. When Pip makes a final sacrifice for Magwitch, we realize that Pip has at last acted for himself out of motives other than fear or ambition. This final reversal of our expectations about what will happen in the book—for Pip has given up his great expectations of wealth in order to save the very man whom we had earlier hoped would be returned to prison or done in—and the modification in our desires for Pip, and the reversal of the fairy-tale pattern—have all led us toward an appreciation of the meaning of Pip's experience: that ultimately the most important values are those of compassion for other people, of forgiveness and sacrifice.

By pausing periodically, as I have suggested, to ask ourselves what anticipations we have about the course of affairs in the novel, we can become more conscious of these shifts in our attitudes and what the novelist is trying to steer us toward. Hence we gain a sharper insight into the writer's intention. We can also evaluate the *craft* of the novelist. If we feel that we have been wrenched into new attitudes about, say, what Pip's goals in life should be, or if the modifications in our desires or expectations do not derive naturally out of the human situation, we will not be persuaded that Pip, if he were a "real" human being, would have changed his values and goals. We may well have identified a structural flaw in the novel. Certainly, we must be ready to modify our desires and expectations, for that is how we are brought by the novelist to new understandings of experience, but we must also be convinced that the events and the human psychology depicted in the novel would have brought about those modifications. Otherwise we tend to come to the conclusion that the structure of the book is artificial, or that a theme is being crudely imposed upon us. If Dickens' portrait of London life had not been compelling, if he had not created vivid characters who all too clearly represented the evils that Pip's original ambitions were leading him into, if he had not drawn out our sympathy for Joe and other good characters, we would not be willing to accept the attitudes that Pip ends up with as the ones that are right and ring true under the circumstances.

This does not mean, of course, that we must share Dickens' values entirely. Modern readers are less likely than Dickens to be convinced of the power of individual self-sacrifice to reform society. But we should be convinced by the way Dickens has engineered the movement toward those values. Thus, attention to structure, to our expectations and desires or anxieties, can give us a basis for intelligent criticism of a novel.

Great Expectations, for all the skill and complexity it displays, has some structural problems. Dickens could not end it. The novel has been passed on to us with two endings, neither of which is satisfying in the opinion of most readers. Of course the novel is partly autobiographical—Dickens wrote it to try to come to terms with aspects of his own experience—and it is arguable that he had not attained the level of self-understanding (if any-one ever does attain that level) that would enable him to reach a conclusion. It is also possible that Dickens could not honestly envision an adult life that embodied all of our aspirations for Pip. Fine though the values of self-sacrifice and compassion for others are, we—and Dickens—may feel that they are not enough in real life. Our desires for Pip may well have included more positive happiness, more joy and spontaneity, more opportunity for self-expressive action than he finally achieves. Instead, in both endings Pip gives up all ambition and settles down to a rather humdrum middle-class existence. This, of course, raises its own intriguing issues of critical evaluation, for maybe Dick-ens wanted us to be dissatisfied with the mode of life that finally emerges from the novel. Maybe he was trying to show us that the cost of right action and self-realization in the modern world is very great and may require coming to terms with the loss of certain hopes and possibilities; or, at least, that life in nineteeth-century England offered no rich endings. These are the kinds of issues that are still engaging scholars in critical debate, and our method of structural analysis helps to identify them.

Similarly, our sense of the world of *Great Expectations*—of that evil, grasping, menacing society—is so vivid that it, too, may qualify or contradict the theme of the plot. A world as night-marishly rich in strange events, dark mysteries, and stunning people as Dickens' cannot easily be forgotten, cannot be turned off at the book's end. It burns on in our imaginations and seems to overwhelm any tales of individual efforts, like Pip's, to redeem or soften it. Quite often the picture of the world that a novel conveys is too strong for the solutions of the plot. This, too, may furnish us with a standard for evaluating the effectiveness of the structure of a novel. One must be wary, however, of jumping to the conclusion that a novel fails because the individual courses of action that are investigated in it are inadequate to deal with the world that is depicted; not all novels seek resolutions of the ills of society. Sometimes their very theme is that individual ef-forts are fruitless and pathetic. The novel, by its very nature, represents the complexity and variety of human experience from which it takes only an individual slice.

To recapitulate my suggestions for analyzing the struc-ture of a novel: observe what *kind of world* is being rendered, what sorts of activities and events are likely to transpire. Ask yourself periodically what your *expectations* are about the gen-eral shape of the plot—what you think the overall pattern of action is likely to be. Ask yourself also what *desires* or *anxieties* you have built up with respect to the principal characters. Note whether there are two kinds of patterns of expectations: one derived from *real life experience*; another from *traditional plot* or *story formulas*; and inquire of yourself periodically whether they coincide, or contradict each other. In this way you will be able to observe the modifications that you are induced to make in your expectations and desires, and will be able to analyze how they contribute to the meaning of the novel. As well, you will have the basis for intelligent criticism of a novel's structure and of its resolutions of human experience.

It is worth stepping back for a minute to look at the assumptions which underlie our reading of a book like *Great Expectations*. One assumption is that once we understand the motivations and the character of a fictional person like Pip, we can anticipate how he will react to what happens to him in life. Presumably he will react in certain relatively predictable ways to incidents and to his surroundings; that is, how he behaves in moments of stress is determined by his nature and previous experience. We assume also that events and circumstances can change or modify a person's character, as they did with Pip; the crises experienced as one grows up or when one confronts dangers or new situations alter him in certain ways. They may strengthen the will or they may weaken and discourage it; they may relieve fears or they may increase anxieties. Thus there is a kind of interaction between character traits (or personality) and event: personality determines how one will respond to event; event will alter or reshape personality, which in turn will determine responses to subsequent events. This is the basis of a number of critics' analyses of structure, and it works very well with most novels.

There are some novels, however, in which these assumptions are defeated at every turn. Franz Kafka's novel *The Trial*, for instance, opens this way: "Someone must have traduced Joseph K., for without having done anything wrong he was arrested one fine morning. His landlady's cook, who always brought him his breakfast at eight o'clock, failed to appear on this occasion. That had never happened before." There is a knock on the door of Joseph K.'s room and a man he has never seen appears. This man and another stranger inform Joseph K., in a rudely official manner, that he is to get dressed and come with them. Immediately Joseph K. (we are never given his full last name) senses something ominous. With no explanation he has been placed under arrest. There is no crime he recalls having committed; he had offended no one. The situation defies rational explanation:

> Who could these men be? What were they talking about? What authority could they represent? K. lived in a country with a legal constitution, there was universal peace, all the laws were in force; who dared seize him in his own dwelling? He had always been inclined to take things easily, to believe in the worst only when the worst happened, to take no care for the morrow even when the outlook was threatening. But that struck him as not being the right policy here, one could certainly regard the whole thing as a joke, a rude joke which his colleagues in the Bank had concocted for some unknown reason, perhaps because this was his thirtieth birthday, that was of course possible. . . .

When K. asks the men what the charge is, they curtly reply "we don't answer such questions." Later, the "officers" say vaguely that their superiors ordered Joseph K.'s arrest because they " 'are drawn toward the guilty. . . . That is the law. How could there be a mistake in that?' 'I don't know this law,' said K. 'All the worse for you,' replied the warder." How unnerving, to be subject to a law that one knows nothing about. And to be one of those to whom officials are "drawn" because one is "guilty." Yet guilty of what?

Immediately we begin, as with *Great Expectations*, to search for plot patterns in the novel. We formulate our expectations about what will happen. Perhaps this is a frame-up which will be unraveled in the course of the story. Perhaps it is one of those horrible mistakes that governments make, and *The Trial* will be the drama of K.'s struggle to reveal the mistake and prove his innocence. Perhaps K. is actually guilty of a crime, which he has suppressed as he tells the story, and which he will gradually betray, in spite of himself. Our search thus immediately takes us through a catalogue of familiar story situations that come from our previous experiences in fiction or in life, and that enable us to project our expectations about the structure of the novel.

At the same time we are likely to begin to relate the world in this novel to actual, real life social situations. The arbitrariness and absolute authority of the police here suggest that *The Trial* may take place in a totalitarian country—Russia or Nazi Germany. Or perhaps it is a grim prediction of the corporate state of the future. The problem we run into with these speculations, though, is that we are never given enough specific detail, enough description of the place or even the historical period in which *The Trial* occurs, to verify our conjectures. Indeed, the further we go into Kafka's book, the more it seems to be cut off from what is recognizable in our nonfictional world. If we were to use the criteria for modes that I outlined, it would seem that *The Trial* fails to fit comfortably into the mode of the social novel; the life portrayed has very little of the social novel's texture. Yet *The Trial* can hardly be a psychological novel either, for we learn almost nothing about K.'s nature. We are introduced to him at a rather traumatically untypical moment, to be sure, but still we should expect, if this were a psychological novel, to find those traits and bents of mind that would evoke his sensibility filled in. Joseph K.'s is a sparse case history. The vital contexts of family, living patterns, friends, past relationships are all missing. Among other characters, K. behaves impulsively, in a manner that even he finds alarming. The man is in perpetual reaction. K. proves to be neither likeable, as Pip is, nor overwhelming as Henderson often is. Kafka's hero is a strangely neutral figure.

Yet one of the *structural* concepts operative in *Great Expectations* governs the design of Kafka's novel: our anxiety over what will happen to the main character. Despite the haziness of K.'s personality, we feel enough of a general concern for his predicament to read on from mystifying incident to mystifying incident. K. is brought before an Inspector, the man who ordered his arrest, and that man tells him nothing except that he is under suspicion. The Inspector warns K., "don't make such an outcry about your feeling innocent, it spoils the not unfavorable impression you make in other respects." How insidious! Now K.'s conviction of his own innocence is to be made to work against him. The Inspector goes on to assure K. that he may continue with his normal routine, as if nothing had happened. But we know very well that such a thing is impossible to do when one has an unspecified crime hanging over one's head. K.'s life, in fact, goes to pieces before our eyes, as he devotes his energies exclusively to his trial. In consequence, he loses the high position he held at the Bank, and he alienates the people around him through the compulsiveness of his anxiety.

Presumably the trial process will clear things up, one way or another. The function of hearings and trials in Western judicial systems is to explore the nature of the charges and the evidence. Our expectations as readers propel us toward that crucial stage, as one Sunday K. sets off for his "first interrogation."

Joseph K. at this point is still confident enough and sufficiently outraged that he can exercise a little method. Coolly he dawdles on the way to the hearing, so as not to "belittle himself before the Court of Inquiry by a too scrupulous punctuality." The place of the Court, however, turns out to be unmarked. K. finds himself in a street that contains only grey tenements for poor people. His coolness is shattered as the time of the hearing comes and passes without his being able to discover which building holds the Court. Then, almost instinctively, K. enters one of the tenements. The building appears to house only individual flats. No one on the premises claims to know anything about a court. To keep from looking like a fool as he wanders from door to door, K. pretends to be looking for a fellow named Lanz. This is a perfectly understandable deception, but it is not the first, nor will it be the last, time that K. finds himself doing something that is slightly devious or childish, as if he could no longer act in a straightforward manner. Perhaps once one is told that one is guilty, one begins to act like a guilty man.

Finally K. enters a large meeting hall—surely the Court. He is now an hour and five minutes late, but the Examining Magistrate allows the proceeding to go on. The stage on which K. must stand is very crowded; he is afraid that if he moves he will knock the Examining Magistrate off into the audience. The heat and stuffiness are overwhelming. It is hard to see who is in the audience, but there appear to be people from different walks of life. The men and women sitting in the balcony are crammed so close to the ceiling that they must hold pillows over their heads to keep from bumping against it. Clearly the setting in which the hearing takes place is bizarre. Often in *The Trial* we get the feeling that things are slightly askew, as if they took place in a dream.

K. delivers what he considers to be a resounding self-defense, carrying the attack to the authorities, lashing out at them for the skimpiness of their grounds for arrest, appealing eloquently to his audience/jury for support. The crowd responds unpredictably: sometimes cheering K. fervently, sometimes laughing at him, sometimes sitting in sullen silence through K.'s rousing orations. He is uneasy. We are uneasy. Throughout, the official remains essentially indifferent to what K. says. In the midst of one of K.'s brilliant expositions, a woman at the back of the crowd shrieks. It disrupts K.'s train of thought, and the hearing ends. The Examining Magistrate tells K. that "today— you may not yet have become aware of the fact—today you have flung away with your own hand all the advantages which an interrogation invariably confers on an accused man." K. is furious, and we are frustrated.

Frustration may not be the entirely adequate word for our feelings as we read on in *The Trial*. Our anxiety over what will happen to K., which is the dynamic force apparently guiding the structure of the novel, has become by now a larger, vaguer anxiety. It is, first of all, an anxiety about our ability to understand anything in this irrational world where people, especially those in authority, act without apparent motivation, and in which cause and effect do not come into play. Obviously that is the impact that Kafka wants the book to have; he is deliberately working upon our tendency as readers to try to predict what will happen in a novel, what its reasonable course will be, and this tendency rests upon our assumption that the personality of K. and the incidents that he is involved in will somehow interact with each other. But nothing that K. learns, no adaptation that he makes, prepares him for what will happen to him, nor does it even guarantee how he will behave. For, given this world of grotesquely unpredictable events, K. tends to act more and more erratically himself.

This does not mean, however, that we should give up our effort to project ahead the likely pattern of the novel. It means only that we must open ourselves to another possibility: that this is a novel about a world in which an individual's nature and events do not interact in such a way as to mold character or afford us certain insights into human behavior and values, as they did in Dickens' novel. If we were to stop halfway through *The Trial* and ask ourselves what we think the overall pattern of action is likely to be, we would probably conclude there is no discernible, rational pattern. Nevertheless, these questions we ask as we read along help us toward the meaning of the novel, for Kafka's vision of modern life (in a seemingly autocratic country, at least) is that it is capricious and nonsensical in a menacing way.

One of our other principles of novel structure, moreover, might have helped us to reach that understanding of Kafka's meaning earlier. For if we had asked what some of the early episodes of the novel imply about the *kind of world* that Kafka is creating, we would probably conclude that it is a world of irrational, arbitrary activity. Hence, the issue of the nature of the world that is envisioned in the novel can be vital in determining the shape of the book, and, more importantly, what the book wants to transmit to us about human life.

Our expectations regarding the nature of the novel's world assume greater significance as we grow increasingly impatient with K. It is hard to fault some of his moves, but others border on the irrational. Kafka brings us no closer, as the story unfolds, to his protagonist's thinking or nature of mind. Our relationship with the main character of this novel continues to be at arm's length, so that it is difficult to argue that Kafka is maneuvering us by that means. Yet it is almost as if we were involved in Kafka's fictional world in such a way that *we* are being compelled to react to it. The anxiety of a frustrated reading experience converts to an anxiety about the situation that the novel describes. (Here is another of those instances when reader reaction can be put to good use as an insight into interpretation.) K.'s increasing paranoia awakens elements of paranoia in us. By this means a structural principle (our expectations about the nature of the novel's world) leads us into an apprehension of *The Trial*'s mode as that of the novel of symbolic action. For as we anticipate the world to be irrational, frustrating, capricious, and insidious, as we build and fortify those expectations, we enter into a relationship with that world which brings out in us the state of being—insecurity, vague anxiety, paranoia—that is the very subject matter of the novel. We enter what has now become a term in our language: a Kafkaesque situation.

This process, then, is one of running through a kind of checklist of approaches to interpretation. We first try to discover what mode the novel is in: that of the social novel, the psychological novel, the modern romance, or the novel of symbolic action. We can readily exclude *The Trial* from the social mode, given the sparsity of social context, and the apparent absence of cause and effect linkage between events. It will take us longer to make a decision whether Kafka's book is in the psychological mode, because it takes us a while to satisfy ourselves that we will not be shown any more detail about Joseph K.'s nature. Faced with these initial difficulties in assigning the novel to a mode that will enable us to decide what issues to look for, we can begin to apply the principles of novelistic structure to see if they can help us perceive the direction and ultimate objectives of the novel. One principle of structure—our expectations dictated by traditional plot or story formulas—proves useless, for there is hardly anything traditional about the unfolding of events in this book. A second structural principle—our concern over what will happen to the character—is somewhat more useful, for it is what keeps us reading, but even here we are confounded by the vagueness and remoteness of the portrait of Joseph K. We cannot identify closely enough with him to make our concern for him a compelling factor. But the third structural principle—our expectations about the nature of the novel's world—does enable us to put some shape on the book. We discover ourselves in a world of distressing irrationality. As this discovery sinks into us, we begin to respond to that world ourselves. We develop the disquiet, possibly the suspiciousness, that such worlds induce, and suddenly we are partaking of a state of mind or being. *Then* we can identify the novel's mode—that of the novel of symbolic action. The process is complete; we have identified the book's focus and its active structural principles; we can now go on to further interpretation and evaluation of it.

As with *Great Expectations*, we can now use our analysis of structure as a means of evaluating the craft of the novelist. This is not, though, a novel in which the interaction of a character's nature and circumstances produces a pattern of meaning. Joseph K.'s personality, vague as it is, has no bearing on his fate. It is futile to try to evaluate Kafka's novel on the basis of its success or failure in directing us to new ethical insights, when his novel's world defies the causal principles upon which ethics rests. But we can use that very irrational, dreamlike world of the novel as a critical standard. Does it transmit the state of mind in a convincing manner? If we have found ourselves in dreams that have the contours of the world of *The Trial*, or if in real life we have been in a situation where we are made to feel guilty for no reason or thrust into a bureaucratic nightmare which confounds common sense, and if *The Trial* successfully recreates that situation, then the novel has been well crafted. For the critical objective that we should pursue when reading a novel of symbolic action is whether the book has been successful in creating the *effect* of a particular state of being, and not (as in a social novel like *Great Expectations*) whether it has been successful in dramatizing or modifying certain values. In other words, if *The Trial* awakens the anxieties that we might expect to feel in a similar situation, then the novel very likely meets its critical requirements.

The dynamics of almost every novel can be discovered through application of the structural principles I have outlined in this chapter. As we read more widely, we acquire a greater awareness of the nature of various fictional worlds; we accumulate a richer repertoire of story formulas; and we grow more sensitive to the manipulation of our expectations and desires for characters. Such factors have probably been unconsciously guiding our response to novels all along. Authors must assume them if their books are to have their anticipated effect. To bring the factors out of the unconscious state and into play is one of the functions of the taking of notes that we discussed in Chapter 1.

I urge you, therefore, to define in your notes the expectations, desires, and anxieties as they develop, and to record their evolution and modification. This process lays bare the underlying structure of the work. It enables one to see the author manipulating the reader. In the next chapter we shall examine more of those sly manipulations.

Narration and Point of View: Distrust the teller and, sometimes, the tale

4

WE have all seen or heard about mock robberies or staged assaults, used by lawyers or police officers to demonstrate that a half-dozen witnesses to an event will give a half-dozen different versions of it. Reconstructing exactly what happened in a series of swiftly moving actions is surprisingly hard for most of us, but it is scarcely as difficult as attempting to discover or interpret the motives and the emotions of the people involved in the events. We have to rely on guesswork, on surmise, and on what we know of the nature of people, and we do so in the face of the fact that we can never really know the inner thoughts and motivations of others—not even of those individuals we have known the longest. The best we can do is fall back on our own conceptions of why other people act and react, and, like judges or jurymen in a trial, sift through what evidence we have in the way of outward behavior, statements, and relationships that will correspond with our conceptions of human motivation and feeling.

In a novel, presumably, we will have less difficulty in understanding the motives and emotions of characters, and in arriving at a clear picture of what really happened, because the author has refined and focused for us the events, thoughts, or feelings that are most telling and intriguing. A novelist has presumably shut out irrelevant or distracting material (except when complicating a mystery by laying false clues), and has presented— or at least given us the suggestions from which to infer—what we need to know to attain a more complete understanding of the life in the novel. Yet this is frequently not the case. If anything, modern novelists make it harder to discover the true nature of their characters and what actually is supposed to have happened. They do, in fact, seem to engineer us deliberately into ambiguity and confusion. Often we are left, as we were right after reading *Henderson the Rain King*, with the vague, sometimes annoying feeling that the characters don't make sense, and that we never did grasp clearly what took place.

Joseph Conrad's novel *Lord Jim* is a classic modern example of the way in which we are manipulated by the storytellers into this position. I have asked students in several classes to give me any words that come to mind that describe the novel's protagonist, Lord Jim. The list that invariably emerges is wildly inconsistent. The first people to volunteer descriptions usually come up with positive terms such as noble, self-sacrificing, and sensitive. But when some cynical soul suggests that Jim is a coward, all kinds of contradictory descriptions tumble out: defeatist and idealist, hero and weakling. We haggle over the real but difficult distinctions that exist between someone's characterization of Jim as obtuse, and another's that he is naive, or childish. The class may finally lapse into a stunned and dispirited silence when some ambitious soul proposes that Jim is really Christ-like. All the descriptions seem to find ample support in the text, yet they hardly make up a coherent composite portrait. When we ask ourselves how we could have reached such different conclusions about a single character, we can only turn back to the novel, for that reconciliation and validation process I spoke of, and then we gradually discover that the explanation lies to a great extent in the ways the story of Lord Jim has been laid out for us and in the nature of the narrators who have been telling it.

In the first four chapters of *Lord Jim* we watch Jim face three crises. First of all, when he is on a training ship as a young man, a man falls overboard. Jim rushes with the other young trainees to take part in the rescue, but he doesn't quite get to the life boat before it is launched. He is a little chagrined at this, but since the rescue is badly botched—the drowning man is hauled in with a boat hook—Jim, not lacking in self-confidence, comforts himself with the thought that if *he* had saved the man, it would have been more coolly and professionally done.

On Jim's first voyage after training, he is accidentally disabled by a falling spar. The crew ties him to his bunk during a storm at sea, and in his misery he is seized with "shadowy" fears. Uncontrollable rushes of anguish "grip him bodily, make him gasp and writhe under the blankets," and for many horrible hours he experiences a terror that makes him want to escape at all costs. Good weather returns, though, and Jim easily shakes off such momentary self-doubts. His convalescence takes place in a seedy Eastern port, where he idles away his time studying, with a sort of fascination, the drifters and hangers-on—the men of easy principles and no great ambitions—who inhabit those forgotten corners of the Orient. They furnish striking contrasts to the strong, determined, principled young Jim, the son of an English pastor, the epitome of the solid stock that kept England's naval glory—yet they hold an insidious allure for him. When he recovers, he signs on with a crew of such men, but only because it is the first chance he has to get back to Western ports. He is a mate of an ancient, decrepit steamer called the *Patna*, which is taking hundreds of poor Arab pilgrims to Mecca. On the *Patna* Jim faces the most crucial decision of his life.

The first part of the voyage is easy, so that Jim's only pre-occupation is to observe with contempt the incompetence and decadence of his skipper, a vulgar, brutish German, and of his fellow officers, who swagger and boast in drunken and sordid viciousness. Suddenly, on the deadest and quietest of nights, hundreds of miles from shore, the *Patna* grinds with a sickening shudder into a submerged object; its rotten hull caves in. Jim realizes that the *Patna* is doomed and that the chances of saving most of the sleeping pilgrims will be slim, especially in the chaos of terror that would develop as they scrambled for the few lifeboats. He watches helplessly as the other officers scuttle to save their own skins. He now has thrust upon him the awful decision whether to stay with the ship, perhaps to save as many of the passengers as he can, or to flee with the officers before the pilgrims become alarmed. At this crucial juncture, we are suddenly whisked forward by the narrator a month or so in time, to an official inquiry. The *Patna*, we discover, had somehow miraculously stayed afloat and had been towed to safety; Jim and the other officers are now under investigation for dereliction of duty—we later learn that he jumped ship with the rest of them—and the scene describes Jim's somewhat stubborn and resentful attempt to explain the state of things on the stricken *Patna* before he made his decision. Jim is on trial, and we, as readers, are now put in the position of being his jurors—not so much to find out the facts of the *Patna* incident, for those will unfold to us quite clearly, but to weigh the larger, more complicated issues of Jim's moral responsibility and the extent of his guilt for a single, impulsive act.

If the same narrator were to continue to tell us Jim's story from that point on, there would be little doubt about the opinion we would form of Jim. Although that narrator, who is the unidentified, omniscient (or all-knowing) narrator that we most often encounter in novels, does not lay out the incidents of the novel as starkly as I have here (for one thing, he gives us more of Jim's own explanation for his behavior), it seems clear that the first few episodes draw a picture of a man who at best cannot function effectively in times of crisis, and who more likely is flawed with the weaknesses of pride, self-delusion, and cowardice. Indeed, if this impersonal narrator told the rest of the tale in his crisp, cold, and straightforward way, we would probably become increasingly cynical of Jim's pretensions toward greatness. There would be no basis for the kind of ambiguity about Jim's stature that I encountered among my students, and that one encounters among the critics who have written about Conrad's book.

We normally associate such a narrative voice with the author himself, for the voice is not that of a character in the novel; it tells us of things that no character would know, and it articulates, in most cases, the standards or norms by which we assume the author wants us to judge the novel's content. It is, in fact, often referred to as the authorial voice, although more frequently called the omniscient narrative voice. It is unwise to identify this voice completely with the author. From what we know of Conrad, for instance, he is not likely to have considered a young man like Jim as coldly and unequivocally as this narrator does. A number of critics have pointed out that writers do not always speak in their novels as they would speak in letters or in conversations. Writers sometimes cover up their own real attitudes and biases, and often they assume a more incisive, confident manner in their narrative roles. The critic Wayne Booth has concluded that many novelists discover or create a new self when they narrate a novel, a persona who is different from the author himself, and which Booth has called the "implied author." Another scholar of fiction, Kathleen Tillotson, thinks that many authors invent what she calls a "second self," who can say things that the author cannot or would not, and it is this second self who is the narrator.

In any event, we tend as readers to rely upon such an implied author or second self for two things: First of all, we expect him to tell us what actually did happen, or at least what appeared to the characters to have happened, in the novel's world. The omniscient narrator tells no rumors or tall tales and relies on no hearsay without at least warning us that they are rumors or tall tales. In this sense, the omniscient narrator is reliable. Secondly, we depend upon this type of narrator to set up the standards or norms and to articulate the value systems which lead us toward a judgment about a character or an event. This doesn't mean, of course, that we have to share the same standards or value systems. The impersonal narrator in Conrad novels, for instance, has a barely concealed contempt, which we may not share, for many members of the middle class who stay at home and take no risks. And we should be alert, as much as possible, to these imposed value systems, for they are subtly affecting our judgments of characters like Lord Jim. We may very likely be much more sympathetic than Conrad's narrator to Jim's failures. No writer speaks, even as an omniscient implied author or narrator, entirely free of certain biases or blind spots, and without designs on influencing the reader toward certain ways of looking at and evaluating things. All this obviously gets us into the pretty heady business of trying to look behind the supposedly omniscient, reliable narrator, who is set up to guide us through the novel's world, for personal biases and values. And to do this we probably have to know something of the author's own biases and values, which we cannot be expected to do with every book we read. Hence, though we have to keep our own balance and independence of mind while reading a novel narrated by the implied author, we will generally tend to go along with this narrator, knowing that we are learning the truth about what happens in the novel's world, even though we may not entirely concur in the standards by which he is asking us to judge what happens in that world. In the case of Conrad's *Lord Jim*, we can be confident that everything that the narrator recounts in the first four chapters happened in the way it is told to us.

From the beginning of the fifth chapter to the end of the novel, however, the story is told (except for a few short passages) by one of the characters in the novel, Marlow, who is present during Jim's testimony at the Inquiry, and who befriends Jim as the latter tries to live down his disgrace. Now we are less sure that we are getting all the truth, because much of what Marlow will unfold to us was picked up by him from talking with other people, and because we are no longer dealing with the implied author, that reliable narrator who can be presumed to tell us the straight story. Furthermore, we are now getting the facts through the mediation of a man who feels a special, almost protective interest in Jim because he is, Marlow says, "one of us," meaning an Englishman of good stock and high ideals. Nor are the circumstances in which Marlow tells most of his story particularly favorable to unembellished truth, for we are told that Marlow would launch into his monologue perhaps after dinner, on a flower-draped veranda over cigars—a choice setting for a man to spin a good yarn.

Yet the trap I find too many readers of *Lord Jim* falling into is an easy acceptance of Marlow, as if he were as detached, omniscient, and careful with the truth as Conrad's impersonal narrator is. Whenever a character narrates a modern novel, we must listen with the same skepticism and alertness that we employ when we hear a story on the street from a relative stranger, for, from Conrad on, novelists have tended more and more to use character narrators who are unreliable or biased or shortsighted, or who are even out-and-out liars. Our unconscious activity as the jury in the case of Lord Jim is made more difficult because, like jury members, we now must determine for ourselves the credibility of each witness and in this case the chief witness is Marlow.

Marlow turns out to be a sly witness at that. He is garrulous, opinionated, and apparently given to slack generalizations and easy philosophizing. Take these remarks:

> We are snared into doing things for which we get called names, and things for which we get hanged, and yet the spirit may well survive—survive the condemnations, survive the halter, by Jove! And there are things—they look small enough sometimes too—by which some of us are totally and completely undone. I watched the youngster [Jim] there. I liked his appearance; he came from the right place; he was one of us.

This is a slippery passage. For he talks of men being "snared" into doing things for which they get called names or even hanged. In the next breath he speaks of little things that have a devastating effect on certain men. Neither of these situations seems to fit Jim's act in deserting the *Patna* as we understood it; he was neither "snared" into it, nor was it a little thing. Yet Marlow seems to be asking us to think of Jim's case as falling within one of these two conditions, for he next speaks of Jim in this context. Not only that, he is asking us to think not about Jim's moral responsibility, but of the effect of the *Patna* incident upon Jim's spirit. Marlow is sliding us away from judgment about Jim's actions to concern over whether he will be undone; we are still judging Jim's character, but from a much more sympathetic angle. We are also being asked to take a more philosophical view of things, for Marlow likes to talk broadly about the foibles of mankind, and this kind of thinking is inevitably going to smudge over onto our consideration of Jim's case. We are being maneuvered by this man.

Marlow has other devices for setting us up to receive the kind of impression of Jim that he wants us to share with him. Before he describes Jim physically for us, he treats us to the grotesque spectacle of the German captain and the other officers of the *Patna* sulking outside the place of Inquiry:

> . . . I saw [the captain's] monstrous bulk descend in haste and stand still on the outer steps. He had stopped close to me for the purpose of profound meditation: his large purple cheeks quivered. He was biting his thumb, and after a while noticed me with a sidelong vexed look. The other three chaps that had landed with him made a little group waiting at some distance. There was a sallow-faced, mean little chap with his arm in a sling, and a long individual in a blue flannel coat, as dry as a chip and no stouter than a broomstick, with drooping grey moustaches, who looked about him with an air of jaunty imbecility.

Then Marlow renders Jim who is standing with the officers:

> The third was an upstanding, broad-shouldered youth, with his hands in his pockets, turning his back on the other two. . . . This was my first view of Jim. There he stood, clean-limbed, clean-faced, firm on his feet, as promising a boy as the sun ever shone on . . .

Although Marlow's next reaction is resentment that Jim could look so good and still be implicated in the *Patna* incident, he has made us separate Jim from his fellow deserters. That clean-limbed, firm, promising boy cannot possibly be as base as the oily, purple-jowled captain, or the engineer with drooping moustaches and "air of jaunty imbecility."

Marlow is also, as many great raconteurs are, circumlocutious. He bides his time informing us that Jim abandoned the *Patna* in unthinking panic, and before he serves us that vital tidbit of fact, he digresses to tell us about other men's weaknesses. One of those who will judge Jim's action is a Captain Brierly, who, unlike Jim, has distinguished himself by unusual heroism and presence of mind in times of danger. Brierly looks upon Jim during the Inquiry with contempt, yet we soon discover that Brierly killed himself by jumping into the ocean barely a week after the end of the Inquiry, committing, Marlow comments, "his reality and his sham together to the keeping of the sea." If a man of Brierly's stature and self-rigor cannot resolve in his mind the issue of Jim's guilt or responsibility—if it triggers somehow such deep self-doubts that Brierly can only destroy himself—then how can we presume to make harsh assessments of Jim's actions?

Clearly Marlow is introducing factors and is telling his story in such a way that our evaluation of Jim's actions and character is not as clear cut as it might have been if the impersonal narrator simply gave us the incidents directly. We are being manipulated by Marlow, both by the opinions he expresses and by the way he unfolds Jim's story to us. We expect to be manipulated to some extent in reading any novel; all writers assemble their materials with some plan of moving the reader toward certain insights or conclusions. In the case of a novel like *Lord Jim* with a possibly unreliable character as narrator, however, the author expects the wary reader to put up some intellectual resistance, to show some skepticism toward the manipulations of the narrator. Hundreds of thousands of people have probably read *Lord Jim* without being aware that their opinion of Jim has been formed in part by Marlow's arrangement of material and by Marlow's perspective toward Jim. There is nothing intrinsically wrong with this except that such a reader does not get the full complexity and richness that Conrad intended, as I shall show.

Conrad does not make Marlow's vision quite as simple as I have suggested. Although Marlow does, as we have seen, present Jim's case in such a way that we are likely to be much more sympathetic with Jim than if the omniscient narrator had continued to tell us the story, he brings several factors to our attention that cut the other way. For instance, later in his narration Marlow tells of an interview with a French lieutenant who went on board the *Patna* when it was still floating helplessly at sea and stayed aboard the floundering ship while it was towed to port. The French lieutenant matter-of-factly talks about a devotion to one's responsibility as a ship's officer and displays a level of courage that contrasts sharply with Jim's frantic behavior. Marlow himself is a man who has had many close scrapes with death, and who believes in what he calls fidelity to mankind. When Jim at one point tries to make the excuse that there wasn't "the thickness of a sheet of paper between the right and the wrong" of his behavior, Marlow snaps back, " 'How much more did you want?' " Marlow at times says that listening to Jim was like listening to a child.

Marlow also tells his story in two sections. The first section is narrated at a time when Marlow thinks Jim has finally redeemed himself by an act of courage in the Far East and paid the penalty for his disgrace aboard the *Patna*. Marlow is inclined to give Jim the benefit of the doubt, and to maneuver us into looking at Jim in a favorable light. The second section of Marlow's story is told over two years later, when other facts have come to light about Jim that cause further doubt about his regeneration. In this narration, Marlow is more like the omniscient narrator: there is less manipulation of events, less philosophizing, a more direct presentation of the facts. This highlights another aspect of narration by a character: the nature of the narration depends upon the character's knowledge of and attitude toward the incidents described. Like anyone, a narrating character may revise his attitude in response to changed circumstances.

What becomes clear as we go along in *Lord Jim* is that Marlow has a peculiar fascination with Jim's case. Marlow sees in Jim many characteristics of himself, and he wants to know why Jim went bad while he, Marlow, did not. Jim is a romantic and an idealist, and Marlow is curious about the characteristics that would lead such a man to act as Jim does. Marlow wants us to share with him his sense of the complexity of the motives of another human being. Hence Marlow's objective is to produce in his readers the very ambivalence that the responses of my classes to Jim's character indicated.

A study by the scholar John Dozier Gordan of Conrad's manuscripts of *Lord Jim* and of Conrad's sources reveals that much of our reaction to *Lord Jim* adheres to Conrad's intentions.[1] The manuscripts indicate that Conrad was constantly revising the novel in order to influence our judgment of Jim. Gordan points to several instances in which Conrad altered descriptions and narrative language in order to make Jim less unsympathetic than he was originally portrayed. Conrad also played around with the arrangement of material, so we can assume that the effects of Marlow's manipulation were intentionally conceived by the author. We learn, also, that Conrad relied on hearsay, on other people's accounts, and on his own recollections for much of the material that went into *Lord Jim*. The *Patna* incident was modeled on a similar desertion of a ship called the *Jeddah*, of which Conrad had heard second and third-hand accounts, when he himself shipped out to the Far East. The character Jim was inspired by a man, Jim Lingard, whom Conrad met in his travels, and whose swaggering way intrigued him. Since many

[1] *Joseph Conrad: The Making of a Novelist* (Cambridge: Harvard University Press, 1940).

of the incidents that Conrad used for his novel came to him from possibly unreliable sources, and had undoubtedly been altered by the biases and blind spots of numerous tellers, it is understandable that Conrad would find it truer to his own experience to refract Jim's story through Marlow's eyes. Many a modern novelist believes that since no truth comes to us undistorted, and since no one sees another person with complete objectivity, the ways in which incidents are known and character perceived in their novels should reflect that. Hence the use of narrators like Marlow and of shifting points of view.

Conrad was also attuned to the ironies of human life, in which many a self-confident, idealistic young man like Lord Jim deceives himself with his own illusions about his bravery and nobility. Conrad himself, as a young Polish exile, went to sea on a romantic impulse and came to know the differences between high-flown dreams and actuality. A conscious irony may separate the character narrator from the people described: while Jim sees himself acting as a noble, tormented man, Marlow may see him behaving like a stubborn child. Another level of irony emerges from the discordance between our view as readers and Marlow's view, when we understand aspects of Jim to which Marlow seems oblivious.

The discrepancies that arise between our understanding of events or character behavior and the understanding of a narrator like Marlow constitute one of the advantages of having a character tell the story instead of having the omniscient implied author tell it. When we know that the narrator is not shrewd or observant enough, or is too prejudiced, to understand entirely what is happening, we discover the delights of figuring out things for ourselves. We are forced to be judge and jury, to be less passive and to be more alert and skeptical. In a sense we are participating in some of the selection and evaluation that is normally done for us by the novelist. Once we are aware that Marlow, for example, is manipulating the story of Lord Jim to fit his concepts, we may be inclined to rearrange the story mentally ourselves, piece together our own patterns and to amass our own evidence about Jim's case. Since this forces us into speculations about the characters in the novel, we engage, as we did (for slightly different reasons) in reading *Henderson*, in a creative act, and this is exactly what many novelists want us to do. William Faulkner, in his novel *Absolom, Absolom!*, presents us with so many different versions by unreliable narrators of the story of his protagonist Thomas Sutpen that he forces us to recreate the story ourselves. Indeed, the version of Sutpen that may be most true to his character and the facts of his life may be that told by a complete stranger who never knew Sutpen and who had never even been to the South where Sutpen lived. The wry point of this is that our fictions may do more justice to the reality than eye-witness accounts.

Another obvious asset of using a character as narrator is that we get to know that character as well as the characters described. By the end of *Lord Jim*, we have as strong a sense of Marlow—of his beliefs, attitudes, strengths, and weaknesses—as we do of Lord Jim. You cannot listen to the voice of a uniquely defined character like Marlow without feeling his presence. Some authors shift the narrative from one character to another for the comic or ironic effect that grows out of our intimacy with their thoughts. We might observe one character's fancies of what a dashing figure he makes with his elegant mustachios, his flashing smile, his penetrating gaze, his lace handkerchief deftly tucked in his sleeve, and then be shifted to the version of the young woman he is trying to impress, who reflects on his drooping mustache, his rotten teeth, his disgusting leer, and his offensive custom of jamming a dirty handkerchief up his sleeve.

Another effect of using a character as storyteller has already been touched upon: the difficulty of making judgments about people and their motives. Even if we are cognizant of the extent of Marlow's manipulation of us as he tells the story, we have found Jim to be a man more difficult to categorize than we thought while reading the first four chapters. We are made conscious of how susceptible to suggestion we ourselves are, and, what is worse, how burdened we are by our own preferences and values when making judgments about other people. Few readers can deny that they are inclined to think better of a clean, vigorous young man like Jim than of a wheezing, purple-jowled old fraud like the German captain. We are open to all kinds of covert appeals to our prejudices, tastes, and moral principles.

Every writer is sensitive to the preformed attitudes that each reader brings to the reading of a book, and for many a nineteenth and twentieth-century novelist, a function of the novel is to shake up those attitudes. Conrad is not alone in wanting to educate his readers in the complexity—indeed, the near impossibility—of passing judgment on a fellow human being. A recurrent delight of authorship is to toy with readers, to coax their moral indignation or contempt for a character, then tip one's hand so that they see that they have been exploited and suckered into getting foolishly carried away by moral fervor. Vladimir Nabokov's *Lolita* reveals such a writer at play.

The narrator of *Lolita* is a middle-aged, second-rate poet named Humbert Humbert, a convicted murderer and self-confessed child molester. He has a penchant for certain little girls, ages twelve to fourteen, whom he calls nymphets, and his ostensible mission in telling his story is to convince us of the artistic and physical delights of his love for the nymphet Lolita. Most readers, whatever their reasons for reading *Lolita* in the first place, presumably harbor definite moral reservations against sexual exploitation by a middle-aged man of a little girl, and not a few readers (including some prominent critics) have finished the book with a bad taste in their mouths, wondering why a man of Nabokov's talent would waste time on the lecherous fantasies of a dirty old man. Their moral indignation emerges unscathed from the reading experience. A few more readers find their principles at least a bit assuaged by the apparent conversion of Humbert about halfway through the book when his lust changes, so he says, to love for Lolita.

But a surprising number of readers finish the book with fondness for Humbert. Though their moral positions have probably not been permanently altered, they have been made to hold them in abeyance because of their fascination with the character of Humbert himself, much as we were almost converted to affection for Henderson by being made a companion in his hapless adventures. But Nabokov forces this change in our attitudes by an even more clever device: he anticipates our responses and parodies them. Just as we may be registering some distaste for Humbert's florid way of writing, Humbert says "you can always count on a murderer for a fancy prose style." The same thing is true with respect to Humbert's behavior. His supposed reformation is a little too pat, as if the author expected us to see through it. The pattern of his story sounds a bit too much like Dostoyevsky's *Crime and Punishment*, and we notice all kinds of Dostoyevskian characteristics. Similarly, if we are inclined to amateur psychoanalysis of literary characters, we will find that all the Freudian patterns are already planted in the novel for our use. Humbert, in fact, tells us that he has himself read up on psychoanalytical case histories and is a master at imitating the symptoms.

Even more disconcerting, our moral position has been stated for us in a mock "Foreward" written by Nabokov:

> No doubt, [Humbert] is horrible, he is abject, he is a shining
> example of moral leprosy, a mixture of ferocity and jocularity
> that betrays supreme misery perhaps, but is not conducive to
> attractiveness. He is ponderously capricious. Many of his

casual opinions on the people and scenery of this country are
ludicrous. A desperate honesty that throbs through his
confession does not absolve him from sins of diabolical cunning.
He is abnormal. He is not a gentleman.

The "Foreward," which is written entirely in that pedantic, stuffy,
smug tone, is purportedly by "John Ray, Jr., Ph.D."—probably
a college professor somewhere, telling us what to think about
the book. Can we possibly associate ourselves with this opinion?
Can we simply echo the pompous, hidebound moralizing of John
Ray, Jr., Ph.D., whom Nabokov is obviously parodying so well?
If we look thoroughly enough, we will probably find that every
attitude, every literary, moral, psychological, and sociological
interpretation that we might want to bring to this novel has been
anticipated, put in the mouths of fools or Humbert himself, and
we conclude that, unless we are to be made to look foolish ourselves, we must hold off from bringing our handy, preformulated
attitudes to the novel. Parody, of the kind that Nabokov and
other contemporary novelists such as John Barth use, is another
manipulative device designed to keep us from relying too comfortably on our assumptions, and it inevitably makes us more
wary, canny readers, less ready to jump to instant judgments.
On the slick surface of parody we have to scramble to keep our
balance, and we learn to enter into new value-formulating
processes.

The final advantage of seeing the life of a novel through a
character's distorted lens is that it increases the intensity of the
illusion that we are in the novel's world, experiencing it as if it
were real life. We do not have an impersonal, all-seeing narrator
stepping between us and the interreactions of the characters.
The late nineteenth-century American novelist Henry James sub-
stantially influenced the modern shift from the implied author
as omniscient narrator to the character narrator. He was reacting against those garrulous implied authors who dominated so
many Victorian novels, and who would address us as "dear
Reader" to advise us not to worry about the heroine: "She will
never marry that scoundrel." James contended that there could
be no intense illusion of life if a surrogate for the author constantly interrupted, persistently reminding us that this was only
a book, after all. Consider, as an example, William Makepeace
Thackeray's farewell salutation to his insipid little heroine, Ame-
lia, in *Vanity Fair*, as we fade away from the scene in which she
is snugly nestled against her stalwart husband: "Grow green
again, tender little parasite, round the rugged old oak to which
you cling!"

Yet, even though we may acknowledge that there are advantages in using a character as narrator, we should not be too hasty in rejecting even such an apparently "old-fashioned" technique as that of the intruding narrator of the Victorian novel. For many of us, there are few characters in fiction who are as delightful to listen to as Thackeray's omniscient narrator in *Vanity Fair*, a man of wit and charm and grace of expression, a man of the world who can catch a character's quirks with a pen stroke. Listening to Thackeray's narrator has been likened to a pleasant afternoon in a posh English club, being entertained by one of the great raconteurs of the century. There are good things to be said for the intrusive implied author as narrator. There are no limitations to the vision of the action or to knowledge of the characters, as there are when a character's narration is used. Thackeray's narrator speaks from ranges of experience that we do not have. Furthermore, he may articulate some of our emotional responses to his characters in a more incisive, and very likely more colorful, way than we could.

Nor do we travel through many a nineteenth-century novel in confusion or doubt about the value judgments that pertain to the novel's world. We build up fewer anxieties about the characters and give into fewer false hopes. Nineteenth-century readers tended to look upon the narrators in their novels as guides and agreeable companions through what was often a lengthy and diverse reading experience. (Novels ran in most cases to three volumes, and often encompassed a wide range of characters and life carried through several generations.) It is doubtful, also, that one becomes less engrossed in a novel in which the narrator reminds us on occasion that we are hearing a story than in one in which the illusion of direct experience is rigorously maintained.

As for intensity of experience, there can sometimes be nothing more gripping than an implied author/narrator speaking directly to us. Listen to Dickens' implied author talking in *Bleak House* of the neglected slum of Tom All Alone's:

> With houses looking on, on every side, save a reeking little
> tunnel of a court gives access to the iron gate—with every
> villainy of life in action close to death, and every poisonous
> element of death in action close on life—here, they lower our
> dear brother down a foot or two: here, sow him in corruption,
> to be raised in corruption: . . . a shameful testimony to future
> ages, how civilisation and barbarism walked this boastful island
> together.
>   Come night, come darkness, for you cannot come too soon,
> or stay too long, by such a place as this! Come, straggling

lights into the windows of ugly houses; and you who do iniquity therein, do it at least with this dread scene shut out! Come, flame of gas, burning so sullenly above the iron gate, on which the poisoned air deposits its witch-ointment slimy to the touch! It is well that you should call to every passer-by, "Look here!"

That narrator has intruded, all right, and he intrudes as if to grasp us by the scruff of the neck and shake us with his angry rhetoric. There is no lack of drama or immediacy in this. He is no character in the novel, no man we can see, but we know that he is *there* and it is to be with him that many a reader for over a century has turned to Dickens' novels.

There is, then, no best way to tell a story. Nor are the experiments with methods of telling a story entirely a post-Jamesian phenomenon. The first English novel, Samuel Richardson's *Pamela*, is told through a series of letters from Pamela, and she is not the most reliable of character narrators—though protesting her innocence, she is a bit of a tease. The kind of parody that we saw in Nabokov's *Lolita* is used in the eighteenth-century novel *Tristram Shandy* by Laurence Sterne. "Unreliable" narrators were often used in the eighteenth and early nineteenth centuries. Ghost stories, for instance, were told by old crones and superstitious country folk who probably made up things and exaggerated for terrifying effect. The accounts that they give us are often passed down through generations, or from teller to teller, altered slightly in the process. When we discussed *Wuthering Heights* in Chapter 2, we noted that the narrators of that novel were highly unsympathetic to what went on between Heathcliff and Catherine: the storytellers were two old gossips. But this kind of unreliable narration in earlier novels is conceived differently from that in Conrad and Nabokov. Permeating the tradition of ghost stories and tales of the supernatural and the uncanny is the assumption that the events described may never have happened. They are highly improbable. Lord Jim's troubled career, and even Humbert's lecherous capers, are probable; they are assumed by the novelist to be a possible reality, not supernatural in any way. Consequently, the objective of a novelist like Conrad or Nabokov is to make us aware of the potential for distortions and manipulations in accounts of actuality. His purpose is to engage us in that judgmental selection process we noted as one advantage of having unreliable characters narrate the story.

The modern interest in character narration occurred at roughly the same time as another development in presenting a story. That development was experimentation in the *point of view* from which events are seen by the narrator. It is important that we understand the difference between *point of view* and *narrator*. The narrator is the person who tells the story to us. The point of view is the vantage from which the events in the story are seen. For instance, Marlow narrates Jim's adventures, but he doesn't see them as Jim saw them. He is not inside Jim's mind, after all, so he cannot give us the impression of what it was like for Jim at the moment when, say, the panic on the *Patna* took place. Nor is he looking over Jim's shoulder as the events happen, observing those events as a person on the scene might have witnessed them. Thus Marlow's point of view is neither Jim's nor that of our hypothetical man on the scene looking over Jim's shoulder. Had Marlow been on the *Patna*, or been able to read Jim's thoughts at the time, he might very well have been less cool and critical about Jim's behavior; he might have experienced the panic, have believed as Jim did that the ship was sinking, and have been so confused that he would not have been able to weigh all the moral issues involved. We know the consequences of the difference in position quite well; how often have we said to an outsider, "You would have felt differently if you had *been there*," or "If you had seen it as I did, you'd think otherwise."

The nineteenth-century French novelist Gustave Flaubert was, as I observed in Chapter 2, foremost among those who wanted the novel to be more artistic by creating the sort of immediacy and intensity that one seemed to get only in poetry. He was instrumental in shaping those two late nineteenth-century and early twentieth-century modes of the novel that I have called the psychological novel and the novel of symbolic action. In both modes the emphasis is upon experiencing events as the participating individual might, sharing the state of being that is the focus of the book, or tracing the movements within a character's mind. To accomplish such objectives, and to give readers a greater sense of realism by bringing them closer to the dramatic experience in his novels, Flaubert began consciously to experiment with shifts in point of view. His great work *Madame Bovary* is entirely narrated by the omniscient narrator/implied author. But the point of view varies considerably. For one thing, it varies in *how* events are seen. We can roughly approximate this variation if we keep in mind the different camera angles that are used in motion pictures. Sometimes, for instance, the camera gives us a restricted vision; we look directly at an object as if through one individual's eyes, and all other, surrounding activity is shut off from our vision as it would be for that individual. In Flaubert's novel such a point of view is used when Emma Bovary looks at her husband Charles at a time when she is falling in love with another man:

> She turned; there was Charles. His cap was drawn down over his eyebrows, and his two thick lips were trembling, which added a look of stupidity to his face; his very back, his calm back, was irritating to behold, and she saw all his platitude spelled out right there, on his very coat.

Of course, something more complex than a camera angle is presented here. We are participating in Emma's impressions about Charles as they form in her mind. The novel's point of view embodies her feelings and thoughts at the moment as well as what she sees. In addition, we are witnessing the *development* of the impression. Never before had Emma conceived of Charles in quite the way she does in this moment. Her revulsion toward her husband unfolds before us. And what *causes* the revulsion unfolds before us. The sequence of impressions and thoughts transpires in our presence: she turns, sees Charles, sees the cap, the thick lips, thinks how stupid a look he has, sees his back, becomes irritated with its calmness, then perceives all his platitude (his banality) "spelled out right there." We have witnessed the drama of the development and fixing of an attitude.

Point of view in fiction can, therefore, give us not only the sense of being there that a limited camera focus can, but it can give us, as the camera cannot, the sequence of thoughts and emotions in the beholder. Similarly, the motion picture can give us the wide angle shot of a panorama, of vehicles in motion over a long road, of the sweep of a countryside. Flaubert does this, also, by bringing us the point of view of the godlike omniscient observer who can see everything. But here, too, the novel's point of view is not simply a visual angle; it is a *quality of knowledge*. Flaubert begins the narration of Part 2 of his novel with not only a grand sweep across a countryside to provide us with a picture of the new village in which Emma and Charles are going to live, but also a sweep across past time:

> Leaving the main road at la Boissière, one reaches the height of les Leux from where the valley comes into view. The river that runs through it has divided the area into two very distinct regions: on the left are pastures, while the right consists of tilled land.
>
> . . .
>
> Up to 1835 no practicable road for getting to Yonville existed, but about this time a cross-road was cut; . . . it is

> occasionally used by the Rouen teamsters on their way to
> Flanders. Yonville-l'Abbaye has remained stationary in spite
> of its "new outlet." Instead of improving the soil they persist
> in keeping up the pasture lands, however depreciated they may
> be in value, and the lazy village, growing away from the
> plain has naturally spread riverwards.

Here the point of view of the omniscient narrator is one that
stresses his omniscience, his ability to know all that is important
in the novel's world, for he can comment on the history of the
area, and he can give us the relevant judgments about the village:
its backwardness, for instance, which has let the rich lands
depreciate.

The omniscient point of view is most common within early
fiction. Novelists following Flaubert, particularly Henry James,
were more interested in the potential for drama and immediacy
of narrower points of view. Not only is the absence of a godlike
perspective truer to human experience, it serves the aesthetic
ideal of engaging the observer in the action and emotional milieu
of the book. The literary critic Percy Lubbock, to whom we all
owe much of our understanding of the nature of point of view,
argues that where the narrator stands apart, detached and all-
knowing, the working of mind and sensibility tends to be too
remote; it exists on a separate plane, almost in a separate time
and circumstance from that of the world described.[2] This is so
even when a character is narrating; Marlow's personality unfolds
in a time and in circumstances set apart generally from those of
Jim's actions. Such a separation can occur as well when the
narrator is a man like Pip in *Great Expectations* telling his own
life story from the vantage point of adulthood. Wisdom urges
us to keep in mind, nonetheless, that such an older way of presenting a story is not necessarily inferior to later, more immediate
points of view; art, after all, *is* supposed to organize experience
as well as dramatize it.

Henry James' sophistication in handling point of view opened
up the possibility for excitement, intensity, and subtlety in observing fictional experience through a character's sensibility. In
James' short story "The Jolly Corner" we involve ourselves so
fully in the character's point of view that we share his confusion
about what is reality and what is his fantasy. We are rapt in his
concentration, and frozen in his horror. Just a brief example
from "The Jolly Corner" will show how this works. Spencer
Brydon, whose point of view is adopted in the story, has come

---

[2] Perry Lubbock, *The Craft of Fiction* (London: Jonathan Cape, 1921).

back to New York from almost a lifetime in Europe to dispose of
some family property, including the home in which he grew up,
now long vacant. Brydon is obsessed with the possibilities of the
life he might have led if he had stayed in business in New York
instead of going abroad. He begins to prowl his old home late
at night in search of the "ghost" of the man he might have been.
Through a subtle process of self-suggestion, he has become
convinced that his potential other self would have been a venal,
selfish, crude man, yet he must find that out. One night, as he
wanders through the empty house, he develops the distinct impression that the ghost of his other self is in the house with him:
doors are open that he was sure he closed. Brydon's nerve fails,
and in barely controlled terror, he hastens down the stairs to the
front hall but stops short when he *seems* to see a figure in the
dimly lit hall. The implied author describes Brydon's impressions
—from Brydon's point of view:

> It was as if there had been something within [the hall]
> protected by indistinctness and corresponding in extent with
> the opaque surface behind, the painted panels of the last
> barrier to his escape, of which the key was in his pocket. The
> indistinctness mocked him even while he stared, affected
> him as somehow shrouding or challenging certitude, so that
> after faltering an instant on his step he let himself go with
> the sense that here *was* at last something to meet, to touch, to
> take, to know—something all unnatural and dreadful. . . .
> The penumbra, dense and dark, was the virtual screen of a
> figure. . . .

You have undoubtedly noticed how carefully James words this
passage, so that it is easily open to the interpretation that this
was only imagined by Brydon: "it was as if there had been something"; "the indistinctness mocked him"; "he let himself go with
the sense that here *was* at last something." These are clues,
perhaps, that Brydon is inventing an ominous shape out of
shadows, possibly out of his own reflection in a glass near the
door, or out of tricks of light, and that he is giving in to his own
powers of suggestion: letting "himself go." Yet we have by this
time shared his point of view so long that we join with him in
experiencing, almost seeing, that shape. We have been looking
for it, just as he was. When we read, we tend to move quickly
over those careful, qualifying statements ("it was as if", etc.)
because we are anxious to see what he sees. Psychic phenomena
are as gripping and terrifying, after all, as physical phenomena.

Brydon makes out the figure to be a man about his own
age, standing with its hands covering its face, as if in shame
over the ugliness and self-corruption that its face will reveal.

Brydon is transfixed with terrified curiosity; the hands over the
face move, open, are dropped, and the figure is revealed to be
more horrible, more disfigured than Brydon could have imagined.
Brydon stands in shock, for this could not possibly be his alternative self. He wavers physically and the menace becomes greater:

> It came upon him nearer now, quite as one of those expanding
> fantastic images projected by the magic lantern of childhood;
> for the stranger, whoever he might be, evil, odious, blatant,
> vulgar, had advanced as for aggression, and he knew himself
> to give ground. Then harder pressed still, sick with the force
> of his shock, and falling back as under the hot breath and
> roused passion of a life larger than his own, a rage of
> personality before which his own collapsed, he felt the whole
> vision turn to darkness and his very feet give way. His head
> went round; he was going; he had gone.

Even in this passage, as you can see, we cannot be sure whether
Brydon imagined the whole thing, or actually saw a person or a
ghost. And it may not matter, for the drama is primarily psychological. James believed that the adventures of the mind produced
as much tension and excitement as those on the physical or
social plane. His method is geared to capturing the drama of
the individual psychic experience, while maintaining enough
control, through the implied author, to expose the ironies that
arise from the caprices, fantasies, and self-induced terrors of
the subjective vision.

Later novelists—James Joyce, Marcel Proust, William
Faulkner, Virginia Woolf—went beyond James in experimenting
with points of view that reflect more faithfully the human mind
at work. They were indirectly influenced by the findings of
modern psychology, and by the writings of philosophers like
Henri Bergson and the American William James, who demonstrated that human consciousness flows in a never-ending stream,
that it is never as coherent and disciplined and ordered as even
James makes it. They found a source of drama, or at least greater
fascination, in the ways that the mind shifted from subject to
subject, from past to present, from fancy to outer reality. As we
discussed in Chapter 2, the *subject* of their novels became the
human mind itself. But they were experimenting with point of
view, also, revealing to us what we have become all too conscious
of, that everyone's view of reality is inextricably involved with
moods, obsessions, degrees of sensitivity, personal caprices.

The results of these experiments confound our problems
of interpreting character and understanding fictional events. In
Joyce's *Portrait of the Artist as a Young Man* we look out on the

world of a small infant who sees a "moocow" coming down along the road to meet "a nicens little boy named baby tuckoo"; in Joyce's *Ulysses* we indulge the erotic fantasies of Leopold Bloom in the red-light district of Dublin; in Virginia Woolf's *The Waves* we try to penetrate the tangled webs of six different minds thinking about the same events; in Faulkner's *The Sound and the Fury* we grope through the jumbled thoughts of an idiot, Benjy, whose sense of time sequence is completely disordered and whose understanding of events is based on no rationality at all. Yet what we lose in ease of reading and in confidence about the events of these novels, we gain in insight into other human minds, and in awareness of the feel and color of things. We come closer to the combination of sensations, memories, unconscious impulses, and personal associations that make up each individual train of thought. We discover the work of art that is the mind, and, as we must with the character narrations of *Lord Jim* and *Lolita*, we create our own imaginative constructs of the world of the novel. Our next task, therefore, is to look specifically at the people in those fictional worlds and the methods of characterization.

Characters: The "Great" Gatsby · Raskolnikov's double

As long ago as Chapter 1 I argued that literature has a special value over other disciplines because it puts ideas in a *human* context. In Chapter 2 I classified the modes of the novel in reference to the kind of information that we get about the people in them: the characters' motives, their social milieu, the states of being that they embody. In Chapter 3 I suggested that our expectations and desires for major characters in novels form one of the structural principles of the genre. And in the last chapter I attempted to indicate what happens when we are forced to try to comprehend the events of a novel through the medium of another person. Obviously everything we talk about in fiction relates to our understanding of the *people* in it. The novel as an artistic expression appears to have as its objective the deeper, richer knowledge of human life. Other expressions offer insight into color and dynamic tensions, as painting and music do, and even other literary forms, such as poetry, may concentrate on language as much as upon an understanding of human life.

Characterization, therefore, is central to the fictional experience. And the principle objective of the creation of characters in novels is to enable us to understand, and to experience, people.

What ultimately proves most valuable to us from reading
Henderson the Rain King is our apprehension of Henderson;
what proves most valuable from reading *Rabbit, Run* is the
opportunity to know Rabbit Angstrom (whatever we may think
of him). This simple fact is often lost sight of in the process of
literary criticism. And, indeed, what I am going to say about
characterization in this chapter also appears to lose sight of that
fact. I am going to show how characterization functions in the
novel to transmit the book's meaning and social texture, and I
am going to discuss in what manner character is rendered in
novels. But I am not going to discuss what each character is
like, as a representative of human life, because almost every
fictional character is unique. Our relationship to him is also
unique. Henderson, Rabbit Angstrom, Quentin Compson, Joseph
K., Lord Jim, Emma Bovary—they are all individualized, however representative they may be of the human condition and
the times in which they live. The American, British, and Western
European novel as we know it rises out of a cultural climate that
values—perhaps above all things—the uniqueness of the individual.

Much as I would like to talk about the Jay Gatsby and the
Raskolnikov whom I know from Fitzgerald's and Dostoyevsky's
novels, I cannot communicate their human quality as richly as
do the novels, for their life is as unique individuals in those
novels. Nonetheless, I can use them to demonstrate the factors
in characterization that enable authors to communicate their
human qualities and guide us to an understanding of the human
themes of the novels. Those factors are the *complexity of the
characterization*, the *attention given certain figures*, and the
personal intensity that a character seems to transmit. The major
characters in a novel are portrayed, and given their prominence,
through these means.

We are naturally interested in complex people. We are
curious to know what makes them tick. As I suggested earlier,
an advantage that the novel has over real life is that it can take
us inside the consciousness of people whom we otherwise could
not fully comprehend. Our attention gravitates to complex characters because our experience in reading and in the world causes
us to expect that events will produce change in character, and
complex people who act from a combination of motives and
emotions are likely to undergo the most marked changes. What
do we care what happens to a dull clod who registers no response
to what befalls him? Lord Jim, in contrast, is of interest to us—
largely because Marlow makes him appear to be a very compli-

cated person: a young man who wants to be heroic but has fatal flaws of hesitation and cowardice, a romantic, an idealist, yet a man given to childishness, a self-punishing man. Were he a simple case, we would soon have lost the appetite for pursuing his career. His complexity dictates his importance for us.

Let us turn to F. Scott Fitzgerald's *The Great Gatsby* to see how complexity and the other factors of characterization are employed to give a character the stature of a major character. (I will adhere to the terms "major character" and "secondary character" in order to distinguish between those of prominence in the novel and those whose function, as we shall see, is largely supportive or projective. Using the terms "hero" and "heroine" is misleading, because major characters often emerge as something considerably less than heroic. I will use the term "protagonist" interchangeably with "major character.") *The Great Gatsby* provides an interesting instance of the working of the factors of characterization, for Jay Gatsby, the figure of the title, enters the novel relatively rarely, yet he dominates it. Nick Carraway, the Midwesterner who (like Fitzgerald) has come East with his naiveté on his sleeve, describes Gatsby on the second page of his narrative as a figure whose fascination lies in his apparent complexities and contradictions:

> If personality is an unbroken series of successful gestures, then there was something gorgeous about him, some heightened sensitivity to the promises of life, as if he were related to one of those intricate machines that register earthquakes ten thousand miles away. This responsiveness had nothing to do with that flabby impressionability which is dignified under the name of "creative temperament"—it was an extraordinary gift for hope, a romantic readiness such as I have never found in any other person and which it is not likely I shall ever find again. No—Gatsby turned out all right at the end; it is what preyed on Gatsby, what foul dust floated in the wake of his dreams that temporarily closed out my interest in the abortive sorrows and short-winded elations of men.

Gatsby is thereby invested with those qualities that draw our curiosity to him and stimulate our imagination. His nature is inconsistency. Carraway lives next door to Gatsby's elegant estate on Long Island, where carloads of the nation's celebrities, the "beautiful people" of the 1920s, congregate each night for lavish parties spilling out onto the lawn. When Carraway first meets Gatsby there, even the moment of greeting transmits the man's enigma:

> He smiled understandingly—much more than understandingly. It was one of those rare smiles with a quality of eternal

reassurance in it, that you may come across four or five times in life. It faced—or seemed to face—the whole external world for an instant, and then concentrated on *you* with an irresistible prejudice in your favor. It understood you just as far as you wanted to be understood, believed in you just as far as you would like to believe in yourself, and assured you that it had precisely the impression of you that, at your best, you hoped to convey. Precisely at that point it vanished—and I was looking at an elegant young roughneck, a year or two over thirty, whose elaborate formality of speech just missed being absurd.

Even when we learn, as Nick does, that Gatsby's personal myth is somewhat shabbier in its origins than his aristocratic aura would suggest—he rose from poverty through a series of semishady operations—and even when we perceive that the myth is somewhat ludicrously self-created—"After that I lived like a young rajah," Gatsby boasts, "in all the capitals of Europe—Paris, Venice, Rome—collecting jewels, chiefly rubies, hunting big game, painting a little, things for myself only, and trying to forget something very sad that had happened to me long ago"—he still persists in our memory as an enigma. Fitzgerald does not dissipate our sense of romanticism in Gatsby's long efforts to make good in order to be able to "recreate the past" and win the golden girl he could never win as an impoverished young man. The fascinations inherent in his idealism resemble those in Lord Jim.

Gatsby proves to be a symbolic character—symbolic of the American dream of the self-made man, and of the romance of Western civilization's grandeur of personal scope that he tries to imitate. Such symbolic significance is largely achieved through Fitzgerald's sleight of hand. Before we learn anything of Gatsby's background and true nature, we are swept into speculation about him. At one of his parties, the guests talk of the legends surrounding him.

> ". . . he was a German spy during the war."
> One of the men nodded in confirmation.
> "I heard that from a man who knew all about him, grew up with him in Germany," he assured us positively.
> "Oh no," said the first girl, "it couldn't be that, because he was in the American army during the war." As our credulity switched back to her she leaned forward with enthusiasm. "You look at him sometimes when he thinks nobody's looking at him. I'll bet he killed a man."
> She narrowed her eyes and shivered. Lucille shivered. We all turned and looked around for Gatsby. It was testimony to the romantic speculation he inspired that there were whispers about him from those who had found little that it was necessary to whisper about in this world.

Fitzgerald manipulates the presentation of Gatsby in such a way that we construct images of him that persist. As readers we never quite lose that image even though we later come to realize that he has relatively little substance—that his significance lies in what he represents to the more complex Nick Carraway.

Fitzgerald brings into play, for the special purpose of establishing Gatsby's stature, another of the factors that determines the importance of a character in a novel: *the amount of attention given him.* In *The Great Gatsby* the attention comes from the other characters in the book. If people in a novel continually talk about a character, we can assume that he is of some prominence in the book's scheme. Similarly, it is a fair assumption that those people whom we observe most often in the novel, whose appearances are frequent, attain the level of preeminence as major characters. This strikes one as a fairly simple proposition, yet it often creates difficulties when writers lose sight of it. There are instances in which a character is given a good deal of attention for part of a novel and then shoved into the background or off scene as attention turns elsewhere. Even so instinctively artistic a writer as Dickens has worked himself into predicaments that required him to dispose of his characters in a summary manner after lavishing great attention on them. The problem recurs more frequently than one might think. There are many bodies stuffed in fictional closets. It is disquieting to the reader, for we build up expectations and desires about all major characters, and we can fairly anticipate that they will perform crucial functions in elucidating the novel's theme. Their dismissal leaves us with those expectations unfulfilled.

The depiction of Jay Gatsby in Fitzgerald's novel also illustrates the third factor in creating major figures: *the intensity that a character seems to transmit.* All people of mystery fascinate us, as Gatsby fascinates those at the party. Our own experience tells us that sometimes people reveal too much of themselves for their own good: they talk too much. We are encouraged to invest people with greater potentiality if we catch only enigmatic glimpses of them. The aura about Gatsby comes from his opaqueness. Carraway remarks that after a musical presentation at a Gatsby party "girls were putting their heads on men's shoulders in a puppyish, convivial way, girls were swooning backward playfully into men's arms, even into groups, knowing that some one would arrest their falls—but no one swooned backward on Gatsby, and no French bob touched Gatsby's shoulder, and no singing quartets were formed with Gatsby's head for one link."

It is one of the paradoxes of the novel that often people

who are incompletely revealed to us acquire stature because of it. We are accustomed, I think, to find the characters in a Jane Austen novel more shallow than those in a Thomas Hardy novel, who are often described as nearly tragic figures. The reason is that Hardy's figures are more opaque, less explained—their intimate patterns of thought and behavior simply blocked out from our view. I call this paradoxical because Austen probably understood her people better than Hardy did: his insight into human nature may have been less penetrating than hers. Mystery lends the illusion of depth to characters.

Such evocation of mystery achieves its effect, of course, only if we attribute intensity to the character. Consider this image of Gatsby: "A wafer of a moon was shining over Gatsby's house, making the night fine as before, and surviving the laughter and the sound of his still glowing garden. A sudden emptiness seemed to flow now from the windows and the great doors, endowing with complete isolation the figure of the host, who stood on the porch, his hand up in a formal gesture of farewell." A classic set piece of the lonely, driven man. Gatsby has stature as a character because, unlike the rest of the Long Island people in the novel, he is a man with a besetting dream: to win the girl he once loved. We learn that all his energy and thought has been bent to this purpose. In our world of ordinary men and women—living ordinary lives, divided, ambivalent, frittering away their time on petty activities, it is inspiriting to contemplate individuals of intensity. They awaken our sense of human potentiality. And if they are evil, they evoke in us intuitions of the dark, obsessive, or simply undescribable aspects of human nature. The modern romance abounds in such figures, the Catherines and Heathcliffs, but they also enter the social and psychological novels. Ahab of Melville's *Moby Dick* is such a creature, almost demonic in the intensity of his pursuit of the white whale. Little of the man's complexity is exposed to us; he looms in our imagination not for the varied richness of his character, but for the obsessiveness of it.

Intensity as a character trait ensnares our attention so effectively that it can replace those other two elements in the creation of major characters: complexity and the attention given them in the book. A dark and driven soul with obscure motivations may appear only fitfully, but will fix our attention as a major figure in the story. In a famous definition of fictional characters, the early twentieth-century novelist E. M. Forster said that there are "flat" characters who are compelled by a set idea in their creator, and "round" characters who embody all the variations and complexities of human nature. Only round characters, Forster said, are "fit to perform tragically for any length of time and can move us to any feelings except humour and appropriateness."[1] Forster was very likely thinking primarily about flat secondary characters—comic types—when he said this, but it has been taken as a critical guideline in some quarters for some time. Our reading experience tells us that the distinction is inadequate and largely untrue. Complexity—the range of human characteristics—is not necessary to create tragic impact upon us. Intensity alone can supply it.

I have emphasized the factors that establish a figure in the novel as a major character because the significance of the experience in the book almost always inheres in such a character. It is the major characters who deserve our fullest attention; if we understand them, we presumably understand the focal experiences of the novel. Raskolnikov, the protagonist in Fyodor Dostoyevsky's *Crime and Punishment*, for example, is a man of great complexity and intensity who occupies much of the attention of the novel. Through his struggles and actions, we come to understand the human problem of the novel. His separation from ordinary life, his infatuation with intellectual theories of the superman, his arrogation for himself of a place above any morality, his warped sense of human values—these gather strength in his troubled mind, driving him to murder. The self-hate and torment that follow, the dissolution of self-confidence, and eventually the breakdown of psychological control are dramatized vividly. Embodied in Raskolnikov's experience are all the insights into human psychology, and the dramatic confrontation of ideas with experience, for which Dostoyevsky's novel is deservedly praised. As we noted in Chapter 3, the major characters in a novel perform a key structural function: upon them we build expectations and desires, which, in modification, shift or establish our values. Hence the effectiveness of most novels depends upon the ability of the major characters to express and dramatize the human issues of the book. We tend to judge the book on the ability of the characters to embody those issues convincingly. If we believe Raskolnikov to be a convincing portrayal of a man obsessed with certain ideas—that is, convincing in the sense that he behaves as an actual person might under the circumstances, or in the sense that his way of feeling or thinking follows the contours of what we might expect in such a situation—then we can say that those ideas have been effec-

---

[1] E. M. Forster, *Aspects of the Novel* (New York: Harcourt Brace Jovanovich, 1927), p. 73.

tively dramatized. Many novels fail because the major characters do not seem to be living the ideas or the experience that we are told they are living. If, for instance, we were simply told by Dostoyevsky that Raskolnikov believed himself to be above morality, and we were given no psychological insights into his way of thinking and feeling, then the moral issues of the novel would only be asserted, not dramatized. Similarly, Dostoyevsky could say that Raskolnikov murdered an old women because he believed her life was worthless, and Dostoyevsky could even show us Raskolnikov wielding the axe, but it would not be a successful dramatization of the moral and psychological issues involved if we did not believe that Raskolnikov convincingly acted from such motives. Dostoyevsky lays an extensive groundwork of insight into, and understanding of, Raskolnikov's nature, so that when he acts, we can appreciate what it means for him to act as he does. To a great extent, major characters are created because only they are given the amplitude and attention to present convincing dramatizations of the human issues of the book. If they fail in this role, the book essentially fails.

One word of caution about this generalization. As people's aspirations exceed their ability to realize them, and as ideas come to be twisted out of shape by circumstances, novelists find it appropriate to show major characters failing to live by their ideas. The contrast between what one thinks one's behavior dramatizes, and what it actually does, gives rise to irony. We observe, for example, the pathetic discrepancy between Gatsby's solemn vision of himself as a noble spirit agonizing over love for Daisy, the woman he cannot have, and the terrible mess that develops when he tries to turn that love into action. We endure an embarrassing confrontation with Daisy's husband, in which Gatsby insists that Daisy never really loved her husband, and is crushed when Daisy confesses, naturally enough, that it wouldn't be true to say she *never* loved her husband. So starts the collapse of the grand scenario that Gatsby had been imagining. The bittersweet purity in which Gatsby fantasized the moment of truth when Daisy would leave her husband for him breaks down into tawdry bickering, confusion, ambiguity. We have acquired enough insight into Gatsby by this time—and into Fitzgerald's fictional world where nothing lives up to its romantic image— to know that Gatsby, like all men, is less than his grand conception of himself. We are prepared for the irony; we stand back far enough to take in the disparity between the ideal and the literal.

Gatsby's comedown is not, in this instance, a failure of the major character to dramatize Fitzgerald's conception. The governing concept of *The Great Gatsby* is in fact that very point: romantic and glorious self-images are fated to be spoiled by crass reality. Hence the ironic difference between what characters think they represent and what we observe them to be does not always signify that they have failed to dramatize the author's ideas effectively. This must be kept in mind. Nor, in this particular case, is the stature of Gatsby as a dominant figure in the novel diminished by that ironic discrepancy, for we are still fascinated with a man who devotes himself with such intensity to imaginary self-splendor.

The failure of a major character to dramatize a novel's issue occurs when we cannot accept the characterization or its enactment of the issue. For many readers, the heroine of *Crime and Punishment* illustrates that problem. Sonia, whom Raskolnikov comes to love, and who prompts his confession and reformation, is, for some readers, too good to be true: an angelic, wistful figure who somehow is supposed to embody the spiritual strengths of Christianity and love. This is a frightful burden for a character to bear, and so difficult to dramatize that it etherealizes an ordinary woman into a saint. Such burdens overwhelmed most of Dickens' heroines, so that they became only pale, wispy reflections of an idea—an idea insufficiently realized (that is, not imaginatively *real*). It may, indeed, account for the relative lack of success in portraying purely good characters in fiction; they never become convincing enough as individuals to carry the thematic weight assigned to them. When such figures interact with more powerful creations, we sense that the dramatization of the issues that the characters embody has failed.

I have been speaking of the burdens that the major characters bear in the novel. It is fair to expect convincing dramatization of the issues of human experience from major characters. As we turn now to *secondary characters*, however, we discover that they perform more limited functions. In order to understand the role of a secondary character, we must identify some of those functions.

The most obvious function of secondary characters is to populate the world of the novel. Since fiction presents human contexts, the secondary characters establish that context. We discover what the time and the society is like by observing secondary characters going about their ordinary business. In the mode of the social novel, such life is important, for an objective of social novels is to portray the social structure and its nature. In *Rabbit, Run*, Rabbit Angstrom's coach, his mother and father, and other minor figures drift in and out of our vision, weaving the texture of small-town American existence. We need only know of them that they are representative, and for purposes of our critical understanding we need only ask what it is of the general quality of life that they illustrate.

Occasionally such representative figures play larger roles in a novel without reaching the importance of a major character. Often we encounter a character who seems to embody the attitudes and way of life that we assume to be average or normal for a person in this society, and whom we cannot say is purely incidental to the unfolding of the story. Such a character may be a friend of the major character in the novel, or one who comes on scene frequently to comment on events or interact with the major characters. Nick Carraway, who is both character and narrator in *The Great Gatsby*, is such a figure. Nick witnesses much of the action in the novel. He reveals enough of himself for us to know his personality, and to conclude that he is probably representative of the average person of his time. His perspective on things is what we would expect most people to share; his morality the standard one. An average or ordinary individual, in other words. Such a secondary character functions as a *point of reference* from which to see Gatsby's greater intensity. Nick's midwestern background furnishes us with a contrast to the frenzy of Gatsby's opulent Long Island, his conservative life-style a contrast to Gatsby's fierce drive that is spinning out of control. "Every one suspects himself of at least one of the cardinal virtues," Nick says, "and this is mine: I am one of the few honest people that I have ever known." I think that we're supposed to take this confession at face value. As narrator and as character, he will epitomize a straighter, less vainglorious approach to experience. American novelists favor such figures as their narrators: Ishmael in *Moby Dick*, Tod Hackett in Nathanael West's *The Day of the Locust*. They furnish good counterpoint to major characters or to novelistic worlds that are intense or bizarre. They are anchors to the common life. And, on occasion, it is the common, muted experience that acquires a special immediacy: Nick Carraway, because of his ordinariness, embodies the poignancy of foolish American aspirations in a way that the aberrational Gatsby cannot.

Other secondary characters operate in a more dramatic fashion: they act as *foils* to the major characters. They interact or clash with the major characters in order to bring out into the open crucial elements of the nature or predicament of those major characters. You recall that Henderson, in Bellow's novel, spends time in Africa with a young tribal ruler, Dahfu, who awakens in Henderson valuable self-knowledge. Dahfu is a secondary character, but in his long philosophical discussions with Henderson he instills in the American a knowledge of the state of *being* rather than that of becoming. Henderson must come to terms with his fear of death. Dahfu compels his reluctant guest to accompany him into the dungeonlike room in which they are alone with a full-grown lioness. Henderson is constricted with fear:

> "Try, better, to appreciate the beauty of this animal," [Dahfu] said. "Do not think I am attempting to submit you to any ordeal for ordeal's sake. Do you think it is a nerve test? Wash your brain? Honor bright, such is not the case. If I were not positive of my control I would not lead you into such a situation. That would truly be scandalous." He had his hand with the garnet ring on the beast's neck, and he said, "If you will remain where you are, I will give you the fullest confidence."
>   He jumped down from the platform, and the abruptness of this gave me a bad shock. I felt a burst of terror go off in my chest.

Here, obviously, a secondary character functions as a foil with a vengeance. There could hardly be a more direct way of confronting a major character with a crisis than to lure him into a lion's den. Dahfu's relationship with Henderson admittedly has more subtle dimensions than this, but it is a vivid illustration of the interaction of a major character and a secondary character designed to bring to the surface a crucial issue of the novel's experience. Dahfu almost instinctively perceives what torments and limits Henderson. Foils seem to have that uncanny ability. A disreputable scoundrel named "Gentleman" Brown in *Lord Jim*, who is as treacherous and cowardly and slimy a figure as ever skulked the sun-baked ports of the East, proves to have a menacing sixth sense about Lord Jim's weaknesses. Brown, caught in one of his acts of villainy, and trying to weasel out of it, strikes inadvertently but lethally at the very weaknesses that Jim had been struggling to subdue in himself. Brown, though ignorant of Jim's abandonment of his duty on the *Patna* when he leapt overboard, unerringly chooses imagery that revives the episode for Jim and saps Jim's newly won strength of will:

> "—and, by God, I am not the sort to jump out of trouble and leave them in a d——d lurch," I [Brown] said. He stood thinking for a while and then wanted to know what I had done ("out there," he says, tossing his head down-stream) to be hazed about so. "Have we met to tell each other the story of our lives?" I asked him. "Suppose you begin. No? Well, I am

sure I don't want to hear. Keep it to yourself. I know it is no
better than mine. I've lived—and so did you though you talk
as if you were one of those people that should have wings so
as to go about without touching the dirty earth. Well—it
is dirty. I haven't got any wings. I am here because I was afraid
once in my life. . . . I won't ask you what scared you into this
infernal hole, where you seem to have found pretty pickings."

It is awesome that Brown, who knows nothing of Jim's past,
can select phrases—"I was afraid once in my life," "I am not
the sort to jump out of trouble and leave them in a d——d
lurch"—that devastatingly characterize the disgrace that preys
on Jim's conscience. In consequence, Jim's self-confidence
shrivels, and he weakly grants Brown an opportunity to escape,
which proves to be simply an opportunity for Brown to commit
further treachery, which in turn leads to Jim's final ruin. It is as
if Brown opened up old wounds that cripple Jim's spirit, just
as Iago plays on Othello's jealousy and pride. The foil, in its
uncanny, insidious ways, confronts the major character with
that character's own potential (or suppressed) weaknesses or
strengths, and prods him into critical decisions.

Another group of secondary characters acts within the
shadow of the major characters, reduplicating, in different ways,
the experiences that engross the novel's principal figures. When
a minor character goes through the same emotional states as a
major character, or participates in a situation that parallels that
of the major character, then the secondary character functions
as an *analogue*. Shakespeare used this technique frequently.
While a grand and difficult romance gripped his major lovers,
often another pair of lovers faced similar or contrasting problems
on a lesser scale. The secondary experience reflected on the
primary one.

Characters functioning analogically often point up facets
or aspects of the action of the major characters. The minor
characters, being generally less complex, or less intense, and
drawn in shallower relief, present what is often only one side
of the experience. Secondary characters are limited in ways that
the major characters are not. They may be less sophisticated, so
that their responses to the experience are less complex and
interesting. They may suffer less. The novelist uses such analogies
to open up the nature of the primary action taking place among
the major figures.

In *Lord Jim*, for instance, Marlow tells of two secondary
characters whose behavior reflects upon Jim's. Captain Brierly,
who sits in judgment upon Jim's cowardice, is discovered shortly

afterward to have committed suicide. Brierly's record for bravery and competence is unsullied; there is no disgrace like Jim's to haunt him. Brierly is incompletely understood by us; we never penetrate his motives as we do those of the major character, Jim. But the enigmatic suicide sheds light on Jim's moral situation, for it implies that perhaps no one is better than Jim at heart. Some are tested and found wanting; some, like Brierly, are never tested. Perhaps Brierly knew that he, too, would fail the test if it ever came, and took another way out. Another secondary character, the French lieutenant who is assigned to ride the *Patna* as it is towed into port, puts Jim's ethical position in a different perspective. The lieutenant displays bravery and devotion to duty in stark contrast to Jim, for had the damaged *Patna* gone down while being towed, the lieutenant would have had no choice but to perish with it. When questioned about his actions, the Frenchman shrugs them off. He admits to being frightened, but stolidly does as he is told—a vastly less complex man than Jim, a follower not a potential leader. This may be Conrad's point: more complex intelligences may cripple themselves with thought; only they wallow in the intricacies of moral and idealistic considerations.

As readers we should be sensitive to these comparisons. The issues of the novel are sharpened by the actions of subsidiary characters. The dimensions of the major characters' actions fall into place from the behavior of those around them. And the potential reach of the primary action is cast forward by secondary characters functioning analogically. In *Crime and Punishment*, we learn of a minor figure, Svidrigailov, who has fatally hurled himself beyond redemption, and lives the nightmare of torment that Raskolnikov faces unless he quickly pulls back from his own destructive course. Svidrigailov, haunted by his moral corruption, writhes through his last hours in a seedy room, dozing on and off in a feverish chill, waking in terror as something seems to run over his arm and leg under the bed covering. He dreams that it is a mouse that he cannot catch, that keeps jumping on him, darting all over his body, down his back and under the shirt. In the horrible night, while the wind howls maniacally at the window, Svidrigailov plunges into another nightmare, this of finding an abandoned five-year-old girl in the park. He dreams that he takes her home for shelter, and then finds that she is changing in appearance: "a sly crafty eye peeped out with an unchildish wink . . . it was depravity, the face of a harlot. . . . [She laughs at him.] There was something infinitely hideous and shocking in that laugh, in those eyes, in such nastiness in the face of a child. . . ." The dream signifies Svidrigailov's total depravity—the loss of all innocence. Svidrigailov himself signifies the potential debasement that awaits the major character, Raskolnikov. Svidrigailov is the analogue of Raskolnikov's soul. He is a "double": an aspect of Raskolnikov, a projected part of him. Doubles are secondary characters who represent the other half of a person—the good or evil potentiality—or who mirror that person but take a potential emotion or state of mind to distorted extremes. They tell us what is latent in a major character's course of action.

In some novels, the latent, potential aspects of the principal figure's position may reside not in one or two analogous secondary characters, but in a variety of minor characters. In Dickens' fiction, the minor figures often compose what I would call a *composite character.* Each is too limited, too grotesque or stereotyped to be realistic in the sense that Brierly and Svidrigailov are. But were we to consider them all together, we would see that they each represent a small facet of the besetting ill of the time. In Dickens we encounter minor figures who are almost under a spell, almost like those blighted figures in fairy tales who have had the witch's curse laid upon them and can act only in stunted, bizarre ways. In *Great Expectations*, you recall, there is a character named Wemmick who has so compartmentalized his life in response to the pressures of the mercantile society, that he is totally impersonal at work, his mouth straight and tight like a mail slot, and then completely different, warm and sentimental, at home after working hours. His employer, Jaggers, protects himself from the incursions of a dehumanizing world by a different pose: that of the insensitive bully, jabbing his accusing finger at everyone, giving no mercy. Yet he harbors, in secret, a fallen woman, for whom he feels great compassion. Both men are incomplete—not fully human in their range of personality characteristics—but considered together they show us the sickness of the time: the danger of dehumanization that Pip, the major character, faces. Minor characters, whom we often call types because of their limited human flexibility and range, and because they are fixed in one eccentric mold of behavior, function to construct a composite picture of the human condition that is at issue in the novel.

Literary critics have a great deal of trouble with types, because the assumption is that a character who is so limited is not realistic. Real people, as we know, are complex, ambiguous people. Yet these critics are often confounded by the fact that *within the novel's world* limited type characters are very real to us, vivid and memorable as people. This paradox may be resolved by our awareness, when reading, that such type characters have simply had some portions of their nature exaggerated and others blocked out, and by our implicit understanding that they are related to the larger, very real human condition that occupies our attention in the novel.

As fiction writers turn in the twentieth century toward the mode of the novel of symbolic action, the question of the completeness and complexity of characters takes on less importance. A state of being dominates novels in that mode, and all that we know, or need to know, about the minor characters (and, often, the major characters) is the aspect of the state of being that they embody. In many instances, the secondary characters are not intended to be lifelike at all, but are *symbolic* or *projections of the mood or condition of mind* that permeates the book. Limited, obsessively single-minded characters can be expected in such fiction. Thus we often encounter in modern novels a cast of grotesques, comic strip types, psychotic specimens, and fantasy projections. Such characters remind us of the minor figures in a Dickens novel, even though Dickens' fiction is in the social mode and not in the single focus of the novel of symbolic action. And, indeed, the secondary characters in many a contemporary novel function much as Dickens' did: as pieces of a large composite picture of the malaise of the time. You recall that in Chapter i I suggested that our appreciation of Joseph Heller's *Catch-22* would be sharpened if we understood why he chose to use comic strip characters such as Major Major Major or Milo Minderbinder. We can now understand that better if we realize that such creations are intended to be facets of a depersonalized human condition. In an absurd universe, with an absurd war going on, absurd characters reflect that state of being, and they shed light on what confronts the principal character, Yossarian, as he tries to keep from being made into a dehumanized part of the war machine.

As we can see, secondary characters function in a variety of ways: as elements of the society that makes up the human context, as average, normal points of reference, as foils to the major characters, as analogues to the main characters, as composite renditions of the human situation, and as symbols of aspects of the governing state of being. Minor characters are too often overlooked, and too often dismissed as filler or as imaginative caprices. We suffer great loss as readers when we ignore the richly complex operation of secondary characters in the unfolding of a novel's meaning and vision. There is another aspect of reading the novel which we are even more likely to neglect, and which is equally essential to understanding the book: that is in the function of *scenes*, or *episodes* in a novel. For this vital topic, turn to the next chapter.

Scene:
Paris fights·
Maule's curse

THE great temptation in literary interpretation of fiction is to operate on the lofty realm of ideas. The classic image of serious discussion about our great works of Western literature is of furiously engaged readers arguing deep into the night, over red wine and numerous cigarettes, about the meaning in novels by Dostoyevsky and Kafka and Conrad and Joyce. Morality, religion, philosophy, human nature, love, death, the decline of Western civilization—the grand topics that engage the great novelists—are what we love to extract from the books and pontificate about. Class discussions in literature courses often pitch themselves onto that high plane, becoming fascinating interplays of mind when they succeed, "a lot of bull" when they don't. Certainly the idea content in good fiction makes its study challenging and rewarding, but exclusive emphasis on that aspect of novels can often cause the critical study of literature to seem, to many people, abstruse and rather forbidding.

As a teacher of literature, I find that it is often difficult to pull class discussions down from the lofty plane of idea into an examination of the specific details of individual scenes in a novel. One would think that I would not have that difficulty, for presumably it is more difficult to discourse on ideas than to describe and analyze the content of a scene—to describe, that is, what the characters are doing or where the action takes place. But many students do not believe that consideration of such ordinary things is significant. They feel that the important issues of fictional interpretation can only be approached on the level of the grand ideas. So, if I ask what is going on in such and such a scene, I sense a great strain developing in the minds of students as they try to heave forth cogent statements of thematic significance. For surely, they assume, I don't mean literally *what's going on*. Yet that is precisely where I think the study of fiction should commence, and why my objective in this chapter is to make you realize how much can be learned from asking straight-forward questions about the content of individual episodes in a novel. As we shall see, the activities and the settings of fictional scenes shape our responses to the book.

Often we neglect a great deal of what goes on in a novel. We become unconsciously selective, and look only for the big dramatic moments, bypassing the scenes that do not appear to be important. We are all aware that there are climactic scenes in works: those in which a revelation or a great confrontation occurs, scenes in which the hero finally tells the heroine he loves her, or in which the hero kills the old lady with an axe. The other, less dramatic scenes are relegated in our minds to secondary status. The people in a novel have to be doing something, after all, and we assume that many of the episodes only function in a preparatory way, allowing us to get to know the characters, or to acquire an imaginative grasp of the circumstances. Every storyteller has to lay a groundwork. Certainly some episodes serve those purposes, but they are also more revealing than we think. The novel is, after all, a presentation of issues in a living context. We can only understand the novel if we look closely at all the selected glimpses of life that the author has chosen to present to us. For what transpires in scenes is vital to the interpretative process. Issues are rarely stated in so many words: they are acted out, *experienced*. The operating principle I urged upon you in Chapter 1—to assume that everything in a good novel is there intentionally and serves the purposes of the novel —applies equally to scenes. To pass quickly and indifferently through them is to miss the vital presentation through life that is the essential method of the novel.

We should, then, raise questions of each episode in the novel: "Why was that episode presented to us?" "How is it different, or like, previous episodes?" And to answer these questions, we have to ask and answer more elementary ones: "Where

does the episode take place?" "What are the characters *doing?*"
"What changes—in attitude, relationship, position—occur?"

Let me give some examples. Ernest Hemingway's novel *The
Sun Also Rises* begins with a series of short, inconclusive scenes.
The first is a brief one at which the narrator and major character, Jake Barnes, joins Robert Cohn and his wife Frances for
dinner in Paris. They talk about going off somewhere for a
weekend trip, and suggest a few places at random. Jake men-
tions that he knows a girl in Strasbourg who can show them the
town. Cohn kicks him under the table. Later, after dinner, Cohn
pulls Jake aside and says:

> "For God's sake," he said, "why did you say that about the girl
> in Strasbourg for? Didn't you see Frances?"
> "No, why should I? If I know an American girl that lives in
> Strasbourg what the hell is it to Frances?"
> "It doesn't make any difference. Any girl. I couldn't go, that
> would be all."
> "Don't be silly."
> "You don't know Frances. Any girl at all. Didn't you see the
> way she looked?"
> "Oh, well," I said, "let's go to Senlis."
> "Don't get sore."

They part and that ends the episode.

In the next chapter, Jake recalls a similarly dissatisfying
encounter with his friend Cohn. In the chapter after that, we
have yet another brief episode, this one in which Jake, bored,
picks up a streetwalker and takes her to dinner, thinking it
would be mildly interesting to do so. It isn't interesting, but at
dinner they meet a group of Jake's American and English
friends, "writers and artists," who suggest that Jake and his
guest join them at a dance. Jake goes along with the idea. Once
he gets there, however, he doesn't like the crowd.

> . . . I went over to the bar. It was really very hot and the
> accordion music was pleasant in the hot night. I drank a beer,
> standing in the doorway and getting the cool breath of wind
> from the street. Two taxis were coming down the steep street.
> They both stopped in front of the Bal. A crowd of young men,
> some in jerseys and some in their shirt-sleeves, got out. I could
> see their hands and newly washed, wavy hair in the light
> from the door. The policemen standing by the door looked at
> me and smiled. They came in. As they went in, under the light
> I saw white hands, wavy hair, white faces, grimacing,
> gesturing, talking. With them was Brett. She looked very lovely
> and she was very much with them.
> One of them saw Georgette and said: "I do declare. There

is an actual harlot. I'm going to dance with her, Lett. You
watch me."

The tall dark one, called Lett, said, "Don't you be rash."

The wavy blond one answered: "Don't you worry, dear."
And with them was Brett.

I was very angry. Somehow they always made me angry. I
know they are supposed to be amusing, and you should be
tolerant, but I wanted to swing on one, any one, anything to
shatter that superior, simpering composure. Instead, I
walked down the street and had a beer at the bar at the next
Bal. The beer was not good and I had a worse cognac to take
the taste out of my mouth. When I came back to the Bal there
was a crowd on the floor and Georgette was dancing with the
tall blond youth, who danced big-hippily, carrying his head on
one side, his eyes lifted as he danced. As soon as the music
stopped another one of them asked her to dance. She had been
taken up by them. I knew then that they would all dance with
her. They are like that.

Brett is the woman whom Jake loves but cannot marry
because he was injured and made impotent in the war. Besides,
Brett is not the marrying type. Jake and Brett nonetheless leave
the dance, ride in a taxi about Paris, then decide to go to the
Cafe Select. At the Cafe they meet a rather absurd but likeable
fat man named Count Mippipopolous, who takes a liking to
Brett. Jakes leaves them and goes home. Later in the evening,
Brett, very tipsy, bursts in on Jake:

I looked at the clock. It was half-past four. "Had no idea
what hour it was," Brett said. "I say, can a chap sit down?
Don't be cross, darling. Just left the count. He brought me
here."

"What's he like?" I was getting brandy and soda and glasses.

"Just a little," said Brett. "Don't try and make me drunk.
The count? Oh, rather. He's quite one of us."

"Is he a count?"

"Here's how. I rather think so, you know. Deserves to be,
anyhow. Knows hell's own amount about people. Don't know
where he got it all. Owns a chain of sweetshops in the States."

She sipped at her glass.

"Think he called it a chain. Something like that. Linked
them all up. Told me a little about it. Damned interesting. He's
one of us, though. Oh, quite. No doubt. One can always tell."

She took another drink.

"How do I buck on about all this? You don't mind, do
you? He's putting up for Zizi, you know."

"Is Zizi really a duke, too?"

"I shouldn't wonder. Greek, you know. Rotten painter. I
rather liked the count."

"Where did you go with him?"

"Oh, everywhere. He just brought me here now. Offered me ten housand dollars to go to Biarritz with him. How much is that in pounds?"

"Around two thousand."

"Lot of money. I told him I couldn't do it. He was awfully nice about it. Told him I knew too many people in Biarritz."

Brett laughed.

"I say, you are slow on the up-take," she said. I had only sipped my brandy and soda. I took a long drink.

"That's better. Very funny." Brett said. "Then he wanted me to go to Cannes with him. Told him I knew too many people in Cannes. Monte Carlo. Told him I knew too many people in Monte Carlo. Told him I knew too many people everywhere. Quite true, too. So I asked him to bring me here."

She looked at me, her hand on the table, her glass raised. "Don't look like that," she said. "Told him I was in love with you. True, too. Don't look like that. He was damn nice about it. Wants to drive us out to dinner tomorrow night. Like to go?"

"Why not?"

"I'd better go now."

"Why?"

"Just wanted to see you. Damned silly idea. Want to get dressed and come down? He's got the car just up the street."

"The count?"

"Himself. And a chauffeur in livery. Going to drive me around and have breakfast in the Bois. Hampers. Got it all at Zelli's. Dozen bottles of Mumms. Tempt you?"

"I have to work in the morning," I said. "I'm too far behind you now to catch up and be any fun."

"Don't be an ass."

"Can't do it."

"Right. Send him a tender message?"

"Anything. Absolutely."

"Good night, darling."

"Don't be sentimental."

"You make me ill."

The Sun Also Rises goes on for a while like that, cutting, as a motion picture sometimes does, from scene to scene, none of them extensively developed, nothing of any consequence really seeming to happen. But let us look back over them, asking our rather elementary questions, and see how much unfolds.

First of all, the *manner* in which the novel is told, through a series of brief scenes, reinforces the impression of fragmented, inconclusive experience. Longer scenes, with greater extension of the interaction of characters, would presumably lead to a greater understanding and more conclusive relationships. Novels made up of long scenes tend to put greater importance on the slow building of human experience, and often indicate that significant change occurs during the interaction of characters. Novels in which the scenes are brief and unsatisfactory transmit the impression that much of the change in attitude and ethical position occurs outside of social situations, in the minds of the characters when they are alone. They emphasize, through their very form, the unsatisfactory abruptness of human contact.

Secondly, the answer to the question, "Where do the scenes take place?" gives us an insight into the lives of the novel's characters. The setting of the episodes—in sidewalk cafes, at seedy dances, in taxi cabs, in furnished rooms late at night— lets us know that there is no community here, no stable culture. Instead, there is a restless, furtive quality to the existence of these expatriates. Jake's first conversation with Robert Cohn reveals that they would just as soon be anywhere else, and that "it doesn't make any difference" where they go: Strasbourg, Bruges, the Ardennes. They have no real roots anywhere.

Such observations about Hemingway's people are deceptively simple and compact—so straightforward, obvious in a way, that we do not recognize their potency. For they induce an attitude toward the characters and their situation that colors our judgments. We will, from now on, be inclined to consider Jake, Brett, and Cohn as aimless, chronically dissatisfied people—perhaps even shallow, certainly restless. Our attitude toward them shapes, in turn, our expectations about them: they will never be in one place long enough to settle down, and never involve themselves with other people long enough to have strong, fulfilling relationships. Their pessimistic fatality about life infects us. All this Hemingway insinuates into the reader from the activities in the brief episodes that he presents at the beginning the novel (when we might have thought he was just establishing "background"), and from the abrupt, inconclusive nature of those episodes themselves. By discussing the scenes as we have, by asking concrete questions about what literally takes place, we identify the sources of our attitudes and expectations; in identifying the sources, we then acquire the basis for more precise analysis of those attitudes and expectations.

As we continue to ask what is going on in these scenes, we intuit even more of the novel's world and its characters. In the first scene, Jake and Cohn get into a slight squabble over Jake's supposed insensitivity to Frances' jealousy. The very fact that the irritation arises from a minor issue illustrates the touchiness and pettiness of the two men. Cohn is too uptight about his wife; Jake is perhaps inconsiderately indifferent to the nuances of the situation. They are two friends who aren't sensitive to each other; two sets of nerves rubbed a bit raw. Again, we undoubtedly assimilated that as we read about it, but unless, through analysis of the scene, we brought the observation out into the open, we would not be able to define just exactly what it is that seems out of joint in their relationship. Nor would we quite realize that one of the issues that is concerning us—and perhaps Hemingway also—is the nature of friendship.

Similarly, if we were to ask what is going on in the subsequent episode, we reinforce our impression of the characters' lives. In that episode Jake picks up a streetwalker for the amusement of it, takes her to dinner, attaches himself briefly to a party of casual acquaintances, goes to a dance that rather disgusts him, has several drinks, runs into his old love Brett, goes off with her on an aimless ride in a taxi through Paris, ends up at another nightspot, then disengages himself from Brett who takes up with a relative stranger. The pattern of movement again tells us something in itself. It chronicles a restless, easily distracted evening's adventure that produces nothing rich or exhilarating for Jake. He begins it bored and ends it depressed. The brief attachment to the streetwalker, like Brett's later brief attachment to the count, further demonstrates the absence of human commitment. Even when Jake and Brett come together their feelings are undoubtedly intense, but the encounter is unfulfilling and painful. Emotional attachment is either casual or bittersweet. Here, too, the manner of presentation further defines the content. How poignant it is to watch the half-desperate movement from dinner to dance to another party, to see Jake vaguely trying to amuse himself, to witness the quick, intense coming together with Brett, and the equally sharp break. How strong a sense of the *tone* of Jake's activities we get when we build up false expectations of something emotionally significant coming out of each venture, and then see each of them fizzle. The stringing out of these frustrating activities creates in *us* a case of the very fatigue and disappointment that Jake feels at the end of the scenes. Led to expect that something significant will occur in each episode, we are let down when nothing consequential does occur. The *structure* of the episodes contributes to the meaning of them. We lose this insight if we distill only general conclusions about the characters, if we do not talk about the episodes and their content in the way we have done.

Attention to the details of each scene yields even more. The way that Jake handles himself is intriguing. He is short in his answers, as if guarded. He is cynical. He is impatient with people. His refusal to hang onto either of the women he is with during the evening underscores his refusal, or perhaps his inability, to become involved. His quality of toughness tinged with sadness is a trademark of Hemingway heroes. They protect themselves by not being sentimental. But they lose something in the process, and their story itself becomes sentimental.

Finally, the nature of the scenes opens up the other critical avenues that we have been considering. We can identify *The Sun Also Rises* as a novel primarily in the social mode from these episodes, and thus anticipate the sort of interpretative issues that will arise. Were the scenes less detailed and lifelike, they might alert us to think about the novel as one in the mode of symbolic action; were they less scenes of outward interaction, they might tell the reader that the novel is in the psychological mode. The quick cuts from episode to episode warn us that a manipulating narrator is at work shaping our sensibilities. And of course the scenes delineate a novelistic world of futile, unsatisfying activity that will shape our vision of the novel and build up its own structural expectations.

There is, then, a wealth of interpretative material to be acquired from what might have seemed to be the most incidental of episodes. Themes emerge from the simplest of human activities, and emerge with *specificity*. We can avoid the sloppy generalities that weaken many discussions of novels, if we define the themes in terms of their concrete expressions. At the same time, the novel emerges as a richer fabric, each element of it counting toward the complex total expression. How subtly the threads of issues can be interwoven into the fabric can be demonstrated in another brief vignette. Jake and Brett, still killing time, are together with Count Mippipopolous later in the novel. The three have been drinking the count's champagne and are rather tipsy. Brett and Jake are "ragging" the count, when he informs them rather curtly that he has been in seven wars and four revolutions. He asks if they have ever seen arrow wounds, then abruptly peels off his shirt to display two white welts under his ribs and two scars above the small of his back, where the arrows came out. Brett laconically remarks, "I say. Those are something." The count adds that he acquired the wounds in Abyssinia, "on a business trip." The nature of a scene of this sort is slightly different from those we previously examined. We have established pretty well by now the pointlessness of the lives of the Paris crowd. This episode at first glance appears to add little more than comic relief. Yet more is afoot than that. The count's absurd pride over his misplaced heroism—"I have been in seven wars and four revolutions"—causes one to question the importance of that kind of activity. One could hardly enlist in seven wars and four revolutions out of principles. A love of violence for its own sake, a mercenary impulse, or a need to prove oneself are more likely motivations. The latter appears to be closest to the case, if we are to judge from the count's manner, for he is a braggart and a show-off, egotistically proud of his arrow wounds. The count makes bravery and boldness ridiculous and slightly unsavory. Another issue is thus subtly interwoven into Hemingway's novel, and another skeptical attitude induced in the reader (in this instance, skepticism about pointless bravado, about false heroism). Much later the count's misdirected boldness is contrasted with the elegant courage of the Spanish bullfighter Romero, and we see how central the issue is in the novel. Hemingway wants us to recognize the values in grace, style, purity of movement. Against the wasted activity of the Paris crowd, their self-destructive loving and drinking, their pettiness and false heroism, is set the self-discipline and grace and pure courage of the ritual of the bullfight, as if to say that it is *how* one lives that matters—how one does things as much as what one does. In contrast with the count's egotistical bragging, Romero maintains dignified reserve.

Had we dismissed the episode of drinking with the count as simply comic relief, we would have lost the particular focus it puts on heroism and style. It is my contention that we would still have half-consciously absorbed Hemingway's point, for our mind always takes in more than we consciously note. But had we not paused to consider the episode as we have, we would have passed over this one clear example that so graphically forms the contrast with the bullfighting scene later and sets the terms of the issue.

Scenes of apparent comic relief, or of retreat into the countryside—scenes that break the pace of action in a novel, or that take place in settings outside the normal social contexts of the work—often highlight the values and the manner of life that is being neglected or corrupted in the main activity of the story. Scenes of this sort are too often ignored, too often treated as if they were only filler or only changes of pace. In *The Sun Also Rises* such an episode of retreat into nature clarifies the values that we have seen emerge in the novel. On the way to the Pamplona Festival in Spain, Jake Barnes takes a side trip with an old friend, Bill Gorton, to fish the mountain streams of the Basque country. As far as the plot of the novel is concerned, the episode is largely irrelevant. Jake and Bill are such old friends, so totally relaxed with each other, that conflict is out of the

question. The scene strikes the reader as simply a pleasant interlude between the anxious orchestration of friction in Paris and
the chaotic crises that will later spill forth in Pamplona. It is
the type of scene that we are wont to skim through inatten-
tively, for it demands very little of us emotionally and is far
different from what we are used to in the novel. Yet its thematic
function is substantial. In describing the simple, familiar act
of fishing and of handling one's catch, the author transmits in
a positive way the qualities of life that have been lost in Paris.

> . . . I put on a good-sized sinker and dropped into the white
> water close to the edge of the timbers of the dam.
> I did not feel the first trout strike. When I started to pull
> up I felt that I had one and brought him, fighting and bending
> the rod almost double, out of the boiling water at the foot of
> the falls, and swung him up and onto the dam. He was a good
> trout, and I banged his head against the timber so that he
> quivered out straight, and then slipped him into my bag.
> While I had him on, several trout had jumped at the falls.
> As soon as I baited up and dropped in again I hooked another
> and brought him in the same way. In a little while I had six.
> They were all about the same size. I laid them out, side by side,
> all their heads pointing the same way, and looked at them.
> They were beautifully colored and firm and hard from the
> cold water. It was a hot day, so I slit them all and shucked
> out the insides, gills and all, and tossed them over across the
> river. I took the trout ashore, washed them in the cold, smoothly
> heavy water above the dam, and then picked some ferns and
> packed them all in the bag, three trout on a layer of ferns,
> then covered them with ferns. They looked nice in the ferns,
> and now the bag was bulky, and I put it in the shade of the tree.

The efficiency and competence with which Jake performs a
relatively simple act contrasts with the wasted motion and absurd behavior of the Paris episodes; the cleanness of the mountain setting contrasts with the sordidness of life in the city. As
readers who have been spun from one heady inconclusive encounter to another in the early portion of the novel, we almost
sense the relief of this mountain interlude. The values are not
articulated, but they are unconsciously inculcated in us, so that
when at the novel's climax the expatriates attempt to debauch
and spoil the restrained, efficient grace of the Spanish ceremony
of bullfighting, we are attuned to the kind of judgments that
Hemingway wants us to make. The apparently incidental scene
of Jake and Bill fishing has transmitted to us, on terms that are
familiar to our own experience, a concrete instance of the grace,
self-control, and quiet competency that Hemingway believes are
crucial to dignified survival in a troubled world.

The scenes that we have been considering can be called *compositional scenes*—scenes that set the pattern of life and its texture, that present or help define the values being examined in the novel. There is one further point I wish to make about the use of compositional scenes before going on to climactic scenes. The novel, like any other extended work of art, acquires a rhythm. The rhythm is established by the nature of the compositional scenes, quickening when the story is told in short, activity-packed episodes of the sort in the Paris section of *The Sun Also Rises*, slowing down when the writer drifts into interludes of pastoral relief such as Jake's and Bill's fishing trip in the mountains. A rhythm is also created by repetition and variation of activities or situations throughout the book. When we note the recurrence of a setting, a course of action, or a relationship of characters that is similar to one that appeared earlier, we find ourselves anticipating a similar pattern of action and meaning. We may even ready ourselves for an emotional response similar to the one that arose in the previous situation. Such fluctuations in response cast our own reading experience into a rhythm.

Perhaps the most commonly repeated pattern in prose literature is that of courtship scenes—lovers coming together and moving apart in a kind of ritualized mating dance. The twentieth-century British writer D. H. Lawrence works an effective variation of this rhythm in order to suggest that the lovers in his novel *The Rainbow* are instinctively guided by a larger natural rhythm controlling all human life. In a memorable scene, a young man and woman are stacking sheaves of grain in the moonlight:

> They worked together, coming and going, in a rhythm, which carried their feet and their bodies in tune. She stooped, she lifted the burden of sheaves, she turned her face to the dimness where he was, and went with her burden over the stubble. She hesitated, set down her sheaves, there was a swish and hiss of mingling oats, he was drawing near, and she must turn again. And there was the flaring moon laying bare her bosom again, making her drift and ebb like a wave.
>
> . . .
>
> And always, she was gone before he came. As he came, she drew away, as he drew away, she came. Were they never to meet? Gradually a low, deep-sounding will in him vibrated to her, tried to set her in accord, tried to bring her gradually to him, to a meeting, till they should be together, till they should meet as the sheaves that swished together.

Obviously there is a rhythm of movement within this scene, but it evokes also a larger sense of the structural rhythm of human behavior, for it reminds us that we are a part of nature, and that nature has its own pulse—of the seasons that determine planting, growth, and harvest, of the tides that sweep with the pull of the moon. Men and women are thus instinctively attuned to this pulse, and that is one of the themes of Lawrence's novel: the affinity of the individual to nature and the ways in which modern man has violated that affinity. Beyond that, a deeper reading pattern establishes itself in *The Rainbow*, for this scene of lovers in the moonlight recalls an earlier scene of an earlier generation of lovers in the moonlight, and both resound through later scenes of young men and women under the moon. Each episode contains echoes of the others, awakening our sense of the repeated situation or motif. And since each is slightly different, we are also conscious of the variation, and from variations come sources of interpretation.

I have dwelt upon compositional scenes and their various potentialities because, as I have said, we are too often inclined to dismiss them. In contrast, the *climactic scenes* of confrontation between the characters, and of great, portentous decisions being made and acted out, are easier for us to notice and consider properly. We are ready for them. Even these, though, require a special kind of sensitivity. So much draws together in crucial scenes, so much comes to a head, that the reader must be prepared to gauge its full impact. In many cases, one can discover in such episodes connections, strains of meaning that reach back deep into the book. Crucial, climactic moments in fiction radiate through the body of a novel, casting light on past activities and values, burning idea and insight deeply into what will come after. The critic Mark Spilka has demonstrated that in some novels there are what he calls "expanding scenes" that embody the tension and the motifs that have been spread out through the novel.[1] Because novels by their very nature are so extended in time and theater of action that they make an encompassing, general interpretation of them difficult and inexact, we inevitably search for those moments in a narrative when everything is presented in capsule form. Occasionally we find such moments, and they are almost always ones of crucial action by the characters.

[1] "Comic Resolution in Fielding's *Joseph Andrews*," *College English*, 15 (1953), 11–19.

Such climactic scenes take different forms in accordance
with the structural concepts of the novel. One finds scenes of
confrontation, for instance, in books in which the governing
structural principle is the tension of our anxiety over a character building up the anger or stress or courage to act. One finds
scenes of union in novels in which our desire is for, say, two
lovers to come together. The climactic scenes in other works
may be moments of communication, of revelation of secrets, of
self-understanding, of freedom. In Nathaniel Hawthorne's famous novel, *The House of the Seven Gables*, the climactic moment would seem likely to be one of release or escape. Through
the early compositional episodes, Hawthorne builds up the oppressive immobility that grips the Pyncheon family, residents
of the Gothic mansion, the House of the Seven Gables. It is suggested that a curse lies upon the family. One of their forebears,
Colonel Pyncheon, had coveted the property on which the house
stands, and had, legend says, acquired it by having the property's
owner, Matthew Maule, burned as a witch. Whatever the spell
of the past, the present day Pyncheons are fallen on bad times.
The house is in partial disrepair, the carpeting worn thin, the
furniture yellowing, and the remnants of the human family are
equally blighted. A malevolent cousin, Judge Jaffrey Pyncheon,
holds the two tenants of the house, a wizened old maid named
Hepzibah, and an effete, febrile young man, Clifford, in a curious
thrall. In large part, of course, it is Clifford's and Hepzibah's own
weakness that victimizes them, for each has been shut off from
the world too long: the man a kind of hothouse flower, a parasitic plant; the woman like an old rose that has been kept too
long under glass. There are, nonetheless, stirrings of movement
—Clifford and Hepzibah try to go to church one morning before
turning back for fear of contact with other people—and two
other characters, untouched by the Pyncheon decay, involve
themselves with Clifford and Hepzibah. The expectations that
structure our interest in the story are two-fold: one the impend-
ing disaster as the curse exercises its power; the other the possible release of Clifford and Hepzibah from their psychic and
spiritual bondage. When Judge Jaffrey Pyncheon suddenly dies,
Clifford and Hepzibah experience an immediate headiness of
freedom, and in a crucial, climactic scene in Chapter 17 of the
novel, they make a dash for the railroad station, as if to escape
the brooding past and begin life anew.

The interpretation of climactic scenes requires that we
make essentially the same inquiries that we have been making
of compositional scenes. It requires that we pause to consider

the significance of actions in the most straightforward way, that we pursue the implications of setting, that we attend to what is being said and done. When Clifford buys a train ticket without any coherent sense of destination, we realize that the flight is half-desperate, grounded in the naive hope that one can escape who one has been by leaving the place where one has spent the past. The train itself is significant. In the nineteenth century, the railroad symbolized movement, the American expansionist spirit, modernity. Clifford's and Hepzibah's existence had been an immobilized one, curiously untouched by modern life; presumably the train symbolizes their initiation into the vital world of the present. Yet the train is only a means for human change; it cannot achieve that change in itself. As the trip progresses, we are struck by the futility of it. Clifford is compulsively talkative. He excitedly launches a conversation with a stranger on the train, but as Clifford carries on heatedly and distractedly about his ideas, the stranger seeks to disengage himself from the conversation. We perceive that indeed the liberation may be all talk, and we note that here, as elsewhere in the book's world, there is an insurmountable barrier between people. Clifford's possibilities of expanding his human contact seem to vanish before him.

The setting, a railroad car in which people, stimulated perhaps by the adventure of travel, become instant acquaintances, accentuates the illusion of Clifford's and Hepzibah's plans. The brightly lit interior of the car, the animated conversation of strangers thrown briefly together, connote the falseness of the two Pyncheons' moment of exhilaration. For it will end at the next train stop. At the beginning of the trip Clifford is strangely animated. He shows a vigor never witnessed in him, but it is, we know, unnatural to him. The narrator likens it to the intoxication of wine, and Hepzibah stares at Clifford from time to time as if he were mad. Even more uncharacteristic is Clifford's brief ability to take command of the situation; it is he who makes the decision to flee. Such a reversal of relationships—for Clifford had previously been completely dependent upon Hepzibah— causes us to be acutely aware of what we had heretofore been observing about him: his parasitic weakness. We apprehend even more vitally how important self-assertion must be to him. But at the scene's end, Clifford exhausts his feeble strength, and tells Hepzibah, "You must take the lead now. . . . Do with me as you will.'" His return to dependence climaxes the abortive effort to create an independent personal existence. We know now that this was his last chance—and it has failed. At the close of the chapter the pair concede defeat; they will return to the House of the Seven Gables.

This is what we expect of climactic scenes: a crisis, a moment of action, a testing. All of a character's aspirations, desires, anxieties, or fears are put on the line. Behavior in the climactic moments reveals more clearly than ever the character's true nature and stature, and capacity for action, sentiment, or imagination. Crucial scenes sharpen our understanding of the qualities of mind or character that may have only been hinted at in the compositional scenes. And presumably a line of development—in plot, in our expectations, in character relationships—culminates.

The scene confirms other motifs of the novel, reaching back and pulling into this one episode much of what composes the meaning of the book. The power of the house and its legend is focused by Clifford's observations that " 'the soul needs air; a wide sweep and frequent change of it. Morbid influences, in a thousandfold variety, gather about hearths, and pollute the life of households. There is no such unwholesome atmosphere as that of an old home, rendered poisonous by one's defunct forefathers and relatives.' " The larger implications of the curse of greedy acquisitiveness in American life are articulated: " 'What we call real estate—the solid ground to build a house on—is the broad foundation on which nearly all the guilt of this world rests. A man will commit almost any wrong,—he will heap up an immense pile of wickedness, as hard as granite, and which will weigh as heavily upon his soul, to eternal ages,—only to build a great, gloomy, dark-chambered mansion. . . .' " We recall the nightmarish unreality of the sequestered lives of Clifford and Hepzibah when she says their experience is like a dream. We encounter again a recurring image of the novel when Hepzibah muses that "she was rather of the vegetable kind, and could hardly be kept long alive, if drawn up by the roots." The tangled, overgrown garden that lies behind the House of the Seven Gables had functioned in previous compositional scenes as an emblem of the family itself: ingrown, entangled, struggling for air, weedy and gnarled in the deeply twisted roots of its arid spiritual soil. The analogue to Hepzibah, and to the Clifford that clings to her, is completed.

In these and other ways, the scene spirals out in allusion to the imagery and thematic concerns of the novel. From such a climactic episode, we can pursue these spirals. A scene of this kind not only presents a crucial test for the characters, bringing their natures and attitudes into sharp focus, but it also guides our inquiry back through the book for its motifs and patterns, and it establishes the framework for what will follow. Equally important, it enables us to work from a specific context of action and situation, which is, as we have noted, the irreplacable advantage of interpreting any fictional scene.

We are now ourselves beginning to sense the subtle interactions of fictional elements, beginning to develop our own tangled garden of motifs, functions, and structural principles. Our attention should finally be turned to what is the most complex, and probably the most powerful, of the elements: the uses of language.

7 Language: Communication· Confusion· Intensification· Emotive resonances

THE medium of fiction is, of course, language. That is well enough understood. Less well understood—or less attended to— is the way that language shapes the experience that we share when reading. Frankly, it is difficult to formulate guidelines that will be useful in interpreting the role of language in telling the story and in communicating the emotive and evaluative content of a novel. The nuances of language are so varied, from book to book and within a book, and the factors so complex—factors such as the denotative (direct explicit meaning or reference) and the connotative (idea suggested by or associated with a word in addition to its direct meaning) aspects of language, sentence rhythms, unconscious sounds, variations in syntax—that all I am going to presume to do here is to "tune you in" to differences in language, and to suggest how greatly the realization of the author's conception depends upon his language.

The novel, as an art form, has often been thought to favor a language that is *communicative*. That is, the words function largely as a medium for transmitting to the reader experiences or ideas within the fictional world. If the operation of language in a novel is largely communicative, then we do not need to look primarily for the rhythms, patterns, and interactions of words and phrases among themselves. We treat words and phrases as functional: they set forth the thoughts in the character's mind, say, or information about what takes place literally in the novel's world. They transmit information and attitudes and even emotions and values in the dimensions in which these things exist in the novel.

The narrative language in *Henderson the Rain King*, for instance, is primarily communicative—indeed, sometimes desperately so. Here is the opening of Chapter 4:

> Is it any wonder I had to go to Africa?
> But I have told you there always comes a day of tears and madness.
> I had fights. I had trouble with the troopers, I made suicide threats, and then last Xmas my daughter Ricey came home from boarding school. She has some of the family difficulty. To be blunt, I do not want to lose this child in outer space, and I said to Lily, "Keep an eye on her, will you?"

The shape of this speech tells us that language is being bent into the rough, solid forms of direct communication. The opening rhetorical question—"Is it any wonder I had to go to Africa?"— is a plain appeal that you understand the speaker's predicament clearly. The expression "to be blunt" is another telltale indication of Henderson's need above all to communicate. His rapid summation, in simple sentences, of his past experiences—"I had fights. I had trouble with the troopers, I made suicide threats, and then last Xmas . . ."—transmits the compulsion of Henderson to explain, to clarify. And he must explain himself in what he hopes will be a logical sequence: "I had fights. I had . . . I made . . . and then. . . ." The rush of such data betrays the immediacy of his emotional distress, and that distress is in itself a fact of the situation that he wants to communicate. Henderson's attempt to be logical and blunt indicates his difficulty (which we noticed before) in piecing together his experiences in a way that makes sense. Here is language being used for a communicative purpose in the most straightforward way.

Yet even within this passage, we can discover occasional uses of language that are not primarily communicative. When Henderson says, vaguely, "I did not want to lose this child in outer space," we understand the emotional situation that he wants to communicate, but our mind also absorbs a new dimension of language. That quick image, of the child lost in outer space, imprints upon our mind, even as we read the passage primarily for information about the character, a kind of unconscious imagery that will subtly shape our assessment of Hender-

son's plight. The language here is figurative, sending out reso-
nances that we apprehend on another level—on the level of what
the imagery suggests to us irrespective of its literal reference.
The second sentence in Henderson's statement, that "there always comes a day of tears and madness," also creates such reso-
nances, and they are of a slightly different kind. Rather than
create an image that carries its own special associations in the
reader, the choice of the words "tears and madness," preceded
by the Biblical phrasing "there always comes a day," evokes the
significance of the Biblical accounts themselves—of hard times,
of endurance, of the inevitability of pain and judgment. We shall
have occasion to explore the uncanny operations of these imagistic and associative kinds of language later.

Primarily, the passage that we have examined from *Henderson the Rain King* illustrates the use of language for directly
communicative purposes. Our assumption that fictional language will be communicative is so strong that we attune ourselves to stresses in the need to communicate and to failures or
insufficiencies of communication. When, as in Henderson's case,
those stresses are pronounced—the poor man blurting out all
the seamy details of his past—we develop perhaps a certain human caution in responding to him. When, as in Henderson's
case, the language appears to be falling short of lucid communication—when he cannot say what he means to say or he says
it imperfectly—we develop an ironic or comic response to the
situation. Irony arises when the author causes the reader to
understand the situation differently from the narrator—when
the reader is made aware of the narrator's incomprehension or
limited insight. As we witness Henderson striving to communicate his situation, and as we gradually perceive that he does not
comprehend it well himself, irony governs our response. Modern
authors establish ironic relationships of this kind between reader
and narrator for a variety of reasons: they give the reader the
satisfaction of superior understanding, thus inducing evaluation
and criticism; they also seem to speak aptly to the modern condition; and they highlight the problem of fictional communication itself—its difficulty, the insufficiencies of language.

Colloquial language—everyday expressions and phrasing—
used by a character narrator like Henderson (or, on occasion,
by an omniscient narrator) often produces irony and comedy.
It creates potentially comic effects because we know from our
own experience that our ordinary conversational speech often
falls short of its objectives. Few of us can talk elegantly and
dramatically enough to have our spoken words do full justice to

what we are trying to convey. We attempt to surmount this by intensifying, by overstating, and there is much of that in Henderson's monologue. The irregular, forced heightening of language to compensate for its imprecision is a frequent source of comedy and sometimes of irony. For how else can we respond to the continued unevenness of control that the rush of colloquial, desperately communicative language betrays?

The potentialities (and limitations) of language influence the choice of narrator. If colloquial self-expression of the kind that Henderson engages in conveys an impression of disjointedness, of confusion, and of variations in control (both of one's language and of the experience one is transmitting), then an author who wants to establish such an impression of a fictional world will choose such a narrator. Because the language of ordinary speech patterns so often sets up irony and comedy, writers of this century who view life ironically or comically lean toward first person character narrations. When Conrad, therefore, wanted to engender confusion and ironic complication about Lord Jim's actions and values, he turned to a narrator, Marlow, whose language, as we have seen, is in form and phrasing philosophical, sometimes flaccid, and meandering. Before that, he used the impersonal authorial narrator, and we can see how different the language of that narrative voice is from Henderson's and Marlow's as we read this description of Jim's companions when he convalesces in an obscure Eastern port from an early injury at sea:

> The majority were men who, like himself, thrown there by some accident, had remained as officers of country ships. They had now a horror of the home service, with its harder conditions, severer view of duty, and the hazard of stormy oceans. They were attuned to the eternal peace of Eastern sky and sea. They loved short passages, good deck-chairs, large native crews, and the distinction of being white. They shuddered at the thought of hard work, and led precariously easy lives, always on the verge of dismissal, always on the verge of engagement, serving Chinamen, Arabs, half-castes—would have served the devil himself had he made it easy enough.

This passage also uses language communicatively. Here the urge to be colloquial or even simple in choice of words, in order to get the message across bluntly, as was Henderson's desire, is not in evidence. The speaker here conveys sure judgments through adroit choices of predicates and adverbs: "attuned," "loved," "shuddered," "precariously." So deft are these cutting insights into the motives of the characters that we can sense the shaping within us, as readers, of the hard instruments of critical dissection. The sentences are grammatically fine. There is a certain coldness in perfect, precise sentence construction, where the words chosen, such as the "distinction of being white" or "always on the verge of engagement," could not be improved upon. The diction is what we call formal, and this, too, compels the reader to react to it as if it were authoritative, for we associate formal diction with someone who is learned and in authority. And the passage is terribly efficient: the sentence, "They had now a horror of the home service, with its harder conditions, severer view of duty, and the hazard of stormy oceans," wraps up all the considerations in succinct parallel phrases which proceed quickly and inexorably one upon the other. Such language, and such phrasing, strikes us as being almost intolerant of people. Crisp and "very British," it seems to contain a sneer of contempt.

Perhaps I am imagining that sneer. But from this illustration, and from the passage in *Henderson the Rain King*, we can observe how readily the mind takes off to erect complementary mental projections from our response to the choice of words and phrasing. At times our responses are almost resonating canyons of memory and emotional reaction—drawing upon our past associations with such language, as well as upon what is being described and talked about. In other cases, the reader's response is almost a quick inhibition, when we put ourselves on guard, say, against formal, authoritative, and too shrewdly judgmental diction, as in the Conrad passage. Ernest Hemingway sought in *The Sun Also Rises* to rid communicative language of its easy tendency to exploit such mental structuring. He wanted to make his prose a transparent, denotative depiction of the thing it described. Writing should, Hemingway contended, transmit "the way it was": the hard truth, without built-in judgments, without clusters of words and ways of speaking that set off long, slow fuses of emotional reaction. When that worked for Hemingway, it produced not only a tough, lean prose but also descriptions that clung tightly to what actually, physically happened, as in this famous description of the movements of Romero the matador in *The Sun Also Rises*:

> Each time he let the bull pass so close that the man and the bull and the cape that filled and pivoted ahead of the bull were all one sharply etched mass. It was all so slow and so controlled. It was as though he were rocking the bull to sleep. He made four veronicas like that, and finished with a half-veronica that turned his back on the bull and came away toward the applause, his hand on his hip, his cape on his arm, and the bull watching his back going away.

The language here is purely communicative, and tailored to the rhythm of the action, speeding up to convey the bull's charge: "each time he let the bull pass so close that the man and the bull and the cape that filled and pivoted ahead of the bull. . . ." Then, at the sentence's end, the words are piled up to freeze that movement into a tableau: ". . . were all one sharply etched mass." We pause for a second on the word "mass," because of the word's underlying visual picture and also because phonetically the broad *a* and the hissing *s* sound hold on. In the next sentence, the *l*'s and *o*'s drag out our reading, slowing the rhythm of the action, and giving that sentence—"It was all so slow and controlled . . ."—the sensation in itself of the rocking motion that Hemingway says it resembled. Finally the cluster of crisp, summary actions at the close—"his hand on his hip, his cape on his arm"—replicates the hauteur of the bullfighter as he draws himself up in triumph.

Hemingway's concern in the novel about the aridity of the expatriate life in Paris and the importance of clean, graceful action dictated the language he used. But he had another objective: to strip his prose of the sentimentality that highly imagistic, emotive writing seemed to produce. To his mind, the burdening of experience with all manner of subjective, romantic implications was a cause of the fuzzy emotionality that had produced so many illusions for his generation, and which was keeping men from seeing things as they actually were. Paradoxically, Hemingway's novels of this period have come to be thought of as highly sentimental: largely, I suppose, from what we know about Hemingway's life and from the poignancy of Jake's and Brett's situation, but also because it appears that we as readers invest even the sparest of descriptions with our emotional responses. The vacuum is filled up with emotive reverberations even when the language does not induce specific patterns of sentiment.

William Faulkner, on the other hand, draws in emotiveness until the prose becomes absolutely thick with it. The opening of the "Quentin section" of *The Sound and the Fury* is delivered as Quentin's reverie:

> When the shadow of the sash appeared on the curtains it was
> between seven and eight oclock and then I was in time again,
> hearing the watch. It was Grandfather's and when Father
> gave it to me he said, Quentin, I give you the mausoleum of
> all hope and desire; it's rather excrutiatingly apt that you will
> use it to gain the reducto absurdum of all human experience
> which can fit your individual needs no better than it fitted
> his or his father's. I give it to you not that you may remember

time, but that you might forget it now and then for a moment
and not spend all your breath trying to conquer it. Because no
battle is ever won he said. They are not even fought. The field
only reveals to man his own folly and despair, and victory is
an illusion of philosophers and fools.

To find oneself thus inside a character's mind is almost enough
in itself to unleash a swirl of feelings, for we know that this is
what occurs in our own minds if we muse about our past, our
parents, the significance of a grandfather's watch. But the
images caught up in that swirl—"the mausoleum of all hope,"
"no battle is ever won"—expand with highly charged responses.
These particular images take Quentin's situation beyond that of
one man's despair to incorporate the grander significance of
death and all human despair. Faulkner believes that Quentin's
state of being is inextricably tied up with cultural burdens—the
decadence of his family, the sickly sweet sensuality of his
Southern environment—and with the modern search for identity. Interwoven with all of the character's personal considerations are these larger elements, and Faulkner's prose reflects
them. The Faulknerian sentence structures—long, slightly pon-
derous, built of constructed phrases that roll out one upon the
other—further contribute to the effect produced by Quentin's
musing upon dark and weighty matters. Language is almost
always emotive rather than purely communicative in Faulkner,
and emotive language, as we have noticed, creates a movement
inward to our thoughts and feelings. So, in addition to communicative language, we encounter in fiction *emotive language* which
one critic, I. A. Richards, defines as language "used for the sake
of the effects in emotion and attitude produced by the reference
it occasions."[1]

Another thing worth noting about writers such as Faulkner
is that they use language to *intensify* the implications of the material. The references to war, death, time, and the past in Quentin's reverie enhance the importance of his position. His case is
made to carry larger significance than that of one depressed
Harvard college boy. The combined effect of the prose's emotive
quality, which sets off reverberations in our own memories, and
of its broader reference to grander concerns, produces in the
reader a serious, intensely felt response to the material. The
solemn intonations of the prose—"I give you the mausoleum of
all hope and desire"—collaborate to this end. Faulkner is a mas-

[1] *Principles of Literary Criticism* (New York: Harcourt Brace Jovanovich,
1961), p. 267.

ter of the prose that reads darkly, fraught with meanings that seem to reach into all history and all humanity's earthly struggle.

The extra dimension of allusions in a text of this sort establishes an undercurrent of meaning in a novel that can become as integral to our understanding of the book as is the book's overt subject matter. Gradually our attitude is suffused with Faulkner's references to heritage and man's fate so that we perceive all that occurs in *The Sound and the Fury* with those references constantly in mind coloring our vision. We read the novel as one that speaks to such larger issues: it is more than the story of one Southern family.

Within most good fiction one can trace an *internal structure* established solely through the language. Sometimes it is a collection of images (e.g., the "mausoleum"—death images in Faulkner's book); sometimes it is a recurrence of words that denote a specific kind of value judgment (e.g., "distinction" in the Conrad passage, which describes a rather rigorous way of thinking); sometimes it is a pattern of grammatical structures that reappear in particular situations (e.g., the rush of simple sentences breathlessly trying to recapture a number of events in the past in *Henderson*: "I had fights, I had . . ."). At times the internal structure I describe is a calculated effect of the writer; more often, I suspect, it is unconscious, a way of thinking. Authors may be only secondarily aware of the imagery and choice of language that they habitually employ. The critic Mark Schorer has suggested the uses we can make of our perception of such a structure. He discovers in a number of nineteenth-century British authors what he calls an "analogical matrix," an inset grid of words and traits of diction which may be "buried or dead metaphors" or aspects of "value assertion."[2] For instance, he finds in Jane Austen's prose consistent use of words whose buried semantic reference is to economics and monetary arrangements: words like "credit," "charge," "value," "gain," "cost." The original reference to economic transactions is "buried" when we use them in other contexts, as when we say, "that act of kindness was to his credit." Jane Austen does not use such words in talking about financial matters, but instead to talk about love and emotional relations. Yet the unconscious choice of such words gives a commercial, bargained quality to human behavior and allows us to intuit the materialistic bent of her fictional world.

[2] *The World We Imagine* (New York: Farrar, Straus & Giroux, 1948), pp. 24–48.

A passage in Hawthorne's *The House of the Seven Gables* reveals another matrix or substructure:

> This impalpable claim [by the Pyncheons to a great tract of forest land], therfore, resulted in nothing more solid than to cherish, from generation to generation, an absurd delusion of family importance, which all along characterized the Pyncheons. It caused the poorest member of the race to feel as if he inherited a kind of nobility, and might yet come into the possession of princely wealth to support it. In the better specimens of the breed, this peculiarity threw an ideal grace over the hard material of human life, without stealing away any truly valuable quality. In the baser sort, its effect was to increase the liability to sluggishness and dependence, and induce the victim of a shadowy hope to remit all self-effort, while awaiting the realization of his dreams.

In this excerpt from the novel one finds several words whose semantic origins or secondary meanings seem to be mercantile; for instance, "inherited," "specimens," "increase the liability," "remit." Of course, wealth is in part the subject of the paragraph, but observe that Hawthorne uses some of these words to talk about human "sluggishness and dependence." Combined with the commercial metaphors are words from what one might call medieval aristocratic sources: "cherish," "inherited," "nobility," "princely," and "grace." Other words, such as "shadowy" and "dreams" are to recur all through Hawthorne's prose. We very likely pay scant attention to these terms, whose metaphoric qualities are now so dead that when we use them we do not connect, say, "baser" with base or nonprecious metals. But they operate on us, nonetheless, and in their own particular combination, so that we intuit how crucial to the Pyncheon's story are money, delusions of aristocratic grandeur, and the shadows of false dreams. And, indeed, the choice of words supports what we learn of the nature of the Pyncheons: the undercurrent of language attunes us to the meaning of the action in the novel.

The twentieth-century Irish novelist James Joyce uses imagistic language of this sort to establish an undercurrent of meaning that he then makes serve him in a different way. Where Hawthorne's matrix of analogy very likely was conscious only in the sense that it seemed, as he was writing, the most appropriate choice of words to express his sense of his characters, Joyce, in the semiautobiographical novel *A Portrait of the Artist as a Young Man* consciously establishes, from the beginning of the work, the connotations that certain words shall bear. The novel's protagonist, Stephen Dedalus, is first shown as a boy who is generally repelled by the physical sensation of wetness. We observe this from his vivid recollection of a bed-wetting incident, and when he is thrown into a ditch of stinking, foul water by a bigger boy. Gradually, also, water comes to be associated with death and thus with the dissolution of the stable personality—a classic symbolic meaning of water in its flux and shapelessness. Joyce so painstakingly establishes these meanings for water that it becomes an overt *symbol*: water stands for physical discomfort and psychological dissolution.

As we follow Stephen's story further, however, we become aware that the symbol changes meanings. Water, particularly the water of the sea, begins in later chapters to stand for the possibilities of change (because the sea changes constantly), of travel beyond Ireland, of freedom. The changes in the symbol parallel changes in Stephen's sensibility. As he grows older, comfort and stability become less important than adventure, change, openness. We can, in fact, understand what emotional transformations are occurring in Stephen by tracing the evolution of the water symbolism. The symbol accretes more implications, almost in itself suggesting the growing complexity of Stephen and the growing ambiguity of life for him. So subtly effective is this parallel communication through the symbol that we can understand what is going on within Stephen by looking at the meanings associated with the water symbol. When Stephen's own thoughts or attitudes are not articulated, maybe not even known to him, we gain an insight into them by analyzing what Joyce says that water symbolizes for him at the time, Thus, at a crucial stage in Stephen's growth he is given the opportunity to join the Jesuit order. Before he can sort out his thinking and feelings about the commitment, we can perceive what his real, inner response is, for Stephen talks of spirituality as "dryness," and we know that this contradicts all that the water symbolism has told us he has come to yearn for: change, openness, adventure. Water had always been associated with sensuality in Stephen: as a boy the association was unpleasant, but we have seen that it assumed a more positive association as he matured. We intuit, as readers, that he will not abandon the sensual at this stage in his life for the abstinence of religious duty. Hence the imagery establishes an undercurrent (to continue the water metaphor) of meaning that carries a complex understanding of the character's state of being for us and that at times flows ahead of what the character is able to perceive about personal experience.

Joyce has taken imagery, which we have found embedded

in the language of some of the other writers whom we looked at, and has abstracted it into a complex set of meanings (and of changing meanings) that we call a literary symbol. The symbol takes on its own life, as it were, and functions openly to shape our reading response. It gathers meanings, as the water symbol in Joyce's novel does, so that whenever we encounter it in the text we think of those meanings. Symbols of this sort are consciously employed in modern fiction to assist us in interpreting the experience of a novel, but those substructures or matrices of imagery and reference and value that we identified in the language of Faulkner and Hawthorne and Jane Austen may function equally powerfully in shaping our response to that experience. Language can thus be made to operate as a continuous or repeated vehicle of interpretation. It can be made to function emotively throughout a novel in several ways: (1) through a suggestive web or matrix established by the choice of words or the phrasing that the author perhaps half-consciously tends to use, as Jane Austen does, in telling the story; (2) through patterns created by the introduction of images or valuative concepts that enhance or intensify the meaning of the book, as when Faulkner enlarges the significance of Quentin's situation by references to death, war, and man's spiritual struggles; and (3) through the use of symbols, abstracted concepts that accrue meanings and implications as they reappear in the novel.

To this point we have assumed that language is supportive —that it is designed, consciously or not, to amplify or intensify the material it pertains to. The impression that we get from the subject matter of a passage (such as, say, of the clean movements of the bullfighter) are enriched by the prose that describes it. But language can also be used as a contrast to the subject matter. The internal references within the prose may actually cut against the impression we would expect to be given of the character or the action. James Joyce was intrigued with these possibilities, and in his great novel *Ulysses* he frequently plays off the language of his narrative against the content. He experiments with numerous prose styles, many of them parodies of the styles of other well-known authors, to illustrate what occurs when apparently incongruous language is superimposed upon subject matter. In one witty episode, he describes a young woman, Gerty MacDowell in the prose of women's glamour magazines, with all its exaggeration, triteness, and sensuality:

> Why have women such eyes of witchery? Gerty's were of the bluest Irish blue, set off by lustrous lashes and dark expressive brows. Time was when those brows were not so silkilyseductive.

It was Madame Vera Verity, directress of the Woman Beautiful page of the Princess novelette, who had first advised her to try eyebrowleine which gave that haunting expression to the eyes, so becoming in leaders of fashion, and she had never regretted it. Then there was blushing scientifically cured and how to be tall increase your height and you have a beautiful face but your nose? That would suit Mrs. Dignam because she had a button one. But Gerty's crowning glory was her wealth of wonderful hair. It was dark brown with a natural wave in it. She had cut it that very morning on account of the new moon and it nestled about her pretty head in a profusion of luxuriant clusters and pared her nails too, Thursday for wealth. And just now at Edy's words as a telltale flush, delicate as the faintest rosebloom, crept into her cheeks she looked so lovely in her sweet girlish shyness that of a surety God's fair land of Ireland did not hold her equal.

The "True Romance" manner of this passage can only ridicule the poor character whose way of thinking it purports to represent. Anyone who borrows her ideas from "the Woman Beautiful page of the Princess novelette," and clings desperately to the quick ways to charm and beauty—"blush scientifically cured and how to be tall"—cannot be very bright. How pathetic the insecurity of a mind like Gerty's, how formulaic all her thinking. And, indeed, Gerty hasn't much more dimension than this, and the setting is a ludicrous moment when the hero of the novel, Leopold Bloom, is leering at Gerty while she pretends not to notice. But the mocking language does not quite demolish the character. In fact, a curious thing happens: as we read, the character of Gerty MacDowell comes alive for us and assumes dimensions. Although the women's confession magazine prose would seem to reduce the humanity of the individual and diminish her into a mushy stereotype, this is not the case. Although we are induced by such prose to make fun of the Gerty Mac-Dowells of life, a poignant affection for them emerges instead. Joyce has performed one of his many tours de force with language. He makes it do things one would never expect: ridicule a character and humanize it at the same time. The reader must hold apparently incongruous responses in suspension, thus making understanding of the person and situation highly complex.

Joyce's experiments demonstrate the creativity of language itself. All good writers seem to find that the meaning of the experience they are trying to record takes its shape—sometimes a different shape from that of its original conception—when put into the plastic materials of the art: language. The twentieth-century British novelist Joyce Cary, in a book called *Art and*

Reality,[3] describes the process of converting an "inspiration" or an idea about experience into language: "For the novelist, in fact, there is not only a huge gap between intuition and concept, the first raw statement, but between that statement and its working out in a story. . . . For the truth is that the work of art as completely realised is the result of a long and complex process of exploration, as well as construction." That exploration takes place in the realm of "how one says it"—the language. Invariably, the language modifies the conception: "For the writer . . . has to deal with language which consists . . . of forms which are also contents. That is to say, they are meanings." The novelist "has to ask himself how the manipulation of words, themselves already charged with meaning, will convey the other larger meaning which is to be his content." Cary says it is even more difficult than that. For not only is the artist trying to put a vision into words that have their own references, their own special meanings gained from centuries of use, but those words must also be assembled in grammatical constructions—"sentence by sentence and page by page"—that support the effect of the artistic conception. As we have seen, language is not just words, but syntax and phrasing—arrangements of words that have their own special powers.

Mark Schorer contends that this challenge enriches great novelists. Technique, he says, is a form of discovery. Not only is one forced to evaluate or think through the accuracy of one's conceptions when putting them down on the page (an agonizing reappraisal we have all had to experience), but one discovers new facets of them. "The virtue of the modern novelist—from James and Conrad down—is not only that he pays so much attention to his medium, but that, when he pays most, he discovers through it a new subject matter, and a greater one."[4] The experience expands in significance as it passes through the language in which it must be expressed. Such an expansion into richer meaning is not for the artist only; it is also there for us, as readers, when the language passes on through to us.

[3] *Art and Reality: Ways of the Creative Process* (New York: Harper & Row, 1958), rptd Anchor Books (New York: Doubleday, 1961), pp. 102, 113.
[4] *The World We Imagine, op. cit.,* p. 10.

Informal
Checklist

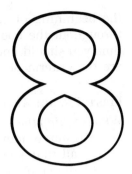

THE idea of what I am about to do—propose an informal checklist of approaches to the interpretation of a novel—is not very attractive to me. If all the considerations of the interpretation of fiction could have been adequately put in such a list, I would not have written the first seven chapters of this book. As I trust you have observed, the elements of critical reading must be explained in detail and must be illustrated through reference to the fictional literature itself. Good novels are highly complex and their effects on various readers even more so. Novels deal with the most subtle and elusive of subjects—human beings—through a subtle and elusive medium: language. And novels take their subjects through change over the course of time, so the picture evolves, is modified, is transformed. Good fiction remains ambiguous: if there were a single, absolute interpretation, a novel would lose its imaginative power and richness.

Now that I have stated some of my misgivings, I offer nonetheless an informal checklist that will help you ask some of the questions essential to the interpretation of the novel. I group the questions in phases to give you some sense of when the issues usually arise, but each novel is different: you may, for instance, want to propound some of the structural questions at the beginning of the novel; or you may find climactic scenes throughout the book rather than toward its conclusion. By this time you should know that openness, flexibility, and shrewdness are the criteria of good critical reading.

FIRST PHASE: In the first few chapters consider these issues:
Who is telling the story?

> An omniscient authorial narrator? He is likely to give you all that you need to know about the circumstances and the characters; he sets the moral norms and is likely to be reliable.

> A character narrator? He is more likely to have limited information and to be biased or unreliable.

What strikes you about the material the author chooses to include?

> What seems to be the primary preoccupation of the author?

> What material is striking or unusual—material that you normally don't encounter in a novel?

> What are your responses to the narrator, the characters, the subject matter, the positions taken in the novel? (Hold these personal responses in abeyance.)

Assuming these early scenes are compositional, what occurs in them?

> What conclusions can you draw from the nature of the activities of the characters—from what they are doing, how they behave, and what they talk about?

> What may be the significance of the setting?

Can you project what this novel will be about? Its likely concerns?
What is the predominant mode of the novel?

> Is this a recognizable society? Are we given detailed descriptions of place, dress, manners?

> Do you get a strong sense of the texture of life in this fictional world?

> Is the focus upon human interaction on the social level?

> *If so,* then the novel is probably one predominantly in the *social mode,* in which you can expect a relatively clear sequence of events, relatively identifiable cause and effect relationships, and you can expect the book to be concerned with ethical problems, social and cultural issues, the relationship of the individual to society.

> *If not,* and if most of the action takes place internally, within the mind of a character or if the material seems to be

organized through the sensibility of a character or characters, then the novel may be in the *psychological mode*,
in which the novel's concern will be with individual
natures and their development, the formation of individual feeling and attitude, and any ethical issues will be
more ambivalent.

Or,

If not, and the author presents little in the way of in-depth
portraits of character and character development; if the
settings are bizarre, unreal, exaggerated; if the characters
are intense, and absorbed with one human concern; then
the novel may be one in the *mode of symbolic action*, in
which states of being and governing ideas are explored
and elaborated.

SECOND PHASE: As you read on in the novel:

*Note material that appears to be inconsistent with your initial
concepts as to the theme of the book, its likely concerns,
its mode.*

Note material that supports your initial concepts.

Note repetitions, patterns, recurring or parallel situations.

Develop the novel's structural principles:

Does the novel seem to be engaging your interest through
your concerns (your desires or anxieties) over what will
happen to the major characters? What expectations do
you have as to what will happen to the major characters
in the course of the book?

Are there any traditional plot or story formulas suggested?
What expectations do these create about the structure
of the novel?

What is the nature of the novelistic world that has been
created? What expectations does such a world give rise to?

Determine the major characters in the novel.

They can be identified as such through the complexity of
their characterizations, the attention given them (by the
author and by the other characters), the personal intensity
that they seem to transmit.

After identifying the major characters, ask yourself what
values, what experience, what ideas, or what sensibilities
the major character or characters seem to be dramatizing.

If this is a novel in the mode of symbolic action, then what
states of being absorb the major characters? Keep in mind

that their actions may be symbolic in the sense that we described, and should not be read literally.

Note the ways in which various secondary characters are functioning:
To establish a social context;
As points of reference for what is normal or ordinary;
As foils, bringing out the weaknesses, strengths, or tendencies of a major character—prodding him to action or insight;
As analogues of the major characters.

Specify the functioning of major and minor characters by analyzing the scenes or episodes in which they appear, noting what they do, what they talk or think about.
Note the points of view from which we observe the characters.

Note the selection and arrangement of episodes, and note what information and what impressions are being transmitted, in order to determine how the author and his agent the narrator are manipulating our reading response. Are events related out of order of their occurrence? What is withheld from us? What is stressed? What is played down?

Are some scenes different enough in setting, in nature, in tone, in content to suggest that they may present alternative values, or different insights into the values or concerns that seem to be dominant in the novel? (E.g., the fishing episode in Hemingway's *The Sun Also Rises*.)

Examine paragraphs closely to determine the use of language.
Is the language colloquial or formal?
Is there ironic or comic failure or insufficiency in communication?
What words recur? What *kinds* of terms (such as commercial terms, nature metaphors, etc.)? What phrasing, what grammatical patterns?
What imagistic language can you observe in the narrative prose? What is its emotive effect?
Have any words or images gathered special meanings and been abstracted so that they become symbols?
Have changes occurred in the language? If so, what is the effect of the change?

Note modifications in structural expectations as they occur.
Note also whether the values or bents of mind that you

think the author is emphasizing have begun to change or be modified by the experiences in the novel or by the author's imagery.

THIRD PHASE: In the latter portions of the book, you should expect to:

Identify climactic scenes:
> Their nature will normally correspond with the issue or problem confronted by the major characters in the novel: they may be scenes of confrontation, union, communication, revelation, attainment of understanding or insight, escape, liberation, defeat, resignation.
> They are frequently times of testing for the major characters, revealing their true natures, their capacities for action, feeling, imagination, suffering.
> Our expectations or desires for the characters are often fulfilled, modified, or defeated here.
>> Does that process accord with what we believe would reasonably derive from the situation or the natures of the people involved?
>> Does it accord with our sense of the novel's world?
>> Does it fit the pattern of any expectations that were dictated by traditional story or plot formulations?
> In what way does the imagery and the human experience in the climactic scene resonate through the novel? What elements are brought together?

Do the matrices of language, or the imagery, reinforce the meaning of the novel's climactic moments? Do they enlarge that meaning? Do they run counter to it?

Reflect upon the end of the novel.
> Why does it end as it does? (I.e., what is the social, psychological, thematic, or aesthetic significance of such a closing of the book's experience and development?)
> What has not been resolved?
> What is the nature of the life that will continue after the novel's end?
> What is the tone of the ending? (E.g., ironic, triumphant, lyrical, gloomy, etc.)

Upon finishing the novel, go back through your notes: relate them to each other; search for complexes of ideas; attempt to reconcile inconsistencies.
> Venture a possible interpretation of the novel.

Validate that interpretation by taking into account apparently inconsistent material.

Bring to bear your own experience, your reading of other fiction.

Bring back into play your own personal responses to the characters and the ideas as a means of gaining perspective on the effect of the reading experience.

In all this, assume that ambiguity remains in any good novel.

Works Discussed in the Text

Jane Austen, *Emma*. 1816; rpt. New York: Norton, 1972.

Saul Bellow, *Henderson the Rain King*. New York: Viking Press, 1958.

Saul Bellow, *Herzog*. New York: Viking Press, 1961.

Emily Bronte, *Wuthering Heights*. 1847; rpt. New York: Norton, 1963

Anthony Burgess, *A Clockwork Orange*. New York: Norton, 1963.

Joseph Conrad, *Lord Jim*. 1900; rpt. New York: Doubleday, 1958.

Charles Dickens, *Bleak House*. 1853; rpt. New York: Heritage Press, 1942.

Charles Dickens, *Great Expectations*. 1860; rpt. New York: Heritage Press, 1937.

Fyodor Dostoyevsky, *Crime and Punishment* (trans. Constance Garnett). 1866; rpt. New York: Heritage Press, 1938.

William Faulkner, *The Sound and the Fury*. New York: Random House, 1929.

F. Scott Fitzgerald, *The Great Gatsby*. New York: Scribner, 1925.

Gustave Flaubert, *Madame Bovary* (trans. Paul de Man). 1857; rpt. New York: Norton, 1965.

John Hawkes, *The Lime Twig*. New York: New Directions, 1961.

Nathaniel Hawthorne, *The House of the Seven Gables*. 1851; rpt. New York: Norton, 1967.

Ernest Hemingway, *The Sun Also Rises*. New York: Scribner, 1926.

Henry James, "The Jolly Corner," 1909, in Leon Edel, ed., *Henry James, Selected Fiction*. New York: Dutton, 1964.

James Joyce, *A Portrait of the Artist as a Young Man*. 1916; rpt. New York: Viking Press, 1964.

James Joyce, *Ulysses*. 1918; rpt. New York: Random House, 1934.

Franz Kafka, *The Trial* (trans. Willa and Edwin Muir). New York: Knopf, 1937.

D. H. Lawrence, *The Rainbow*. 1915; rpt. New York: Viking Press, 1961.

Vladimir Nabokov, *Lolita*. New York: Putnam, 1955.

John Updike, *Rabbit, Run*. New York: Knopf, 1960.

Selected Bibliography

WAYNE C. BOOTH, *The Rhetoric of Fiction*. Chicago: University of Chicago Press, 1961.

CLEANTH BROOKS *and* ROBERT PENN WARREN, *Understanding Fiction*. New York: Holt, Rinehart, Winston, 1943.

E. K. BROWN, *Rhythm in the Novel*. Toronto: University of Toronto Press, 1950.

R. S. CRANE, ed., *Critics and Criticism*. Chicago: University of Chicago Press, 1952.

LEON EDEL, *The Modern Psychological Novel*. New York: Grosset & Dunlap, 1959.

E. M. FORSTER, *Aspects of the Novel*. New York: Harcourt Brace Jovanovich, 1927.

RALPH FREEDMAN, *The Lyrical Novel*. Princeton: Princeton University Press, 1963.

ALAN FRIEDMAN, *The Turn of the Novel*. New York: Oxford University Press, 1966.

MELVIN FRIEDMAN, *Stream of Consciousness*. New Haven: Yale University Press, 1955.

NORTHROP FRYE, *Anatomy of Criticism*. Princeton: Princeton University Press, 1957.

WILLIAM H. GASS, *Fiction and the Figures of Life*. New York: Knopf, 1971.

BARBARA HARDY, *The Appropriate Form*. London: Athlone Press, 1964.

W. J. HARVEY, *Character and the Novel*. Ithaca: Cornell University Press, 1965.

NORMAN N. HOLLAND, *The Dynamics of Literary Response*. New York and Oxford: Oxford University Press, 1968.

ROBERT HUMPHREY, *Stream of Consciousness in the Modern Novel*. Berkeley: University of California Press, 1954.

WOLFGANG ISER, *The Implied Reader*. Baltimore: The Johns Hopkins University Press, 1974.

HENRY JAMES, *The Art of the Novel*. Rpt. New York: Scribner, 1934. *The Future of the Novel*. Rpt. New York: Random House (Vintage Books), 1956.

FRANK KERMODE, *The Sense of an Ending*. New York and London: Oxford University Press, 1967.

SIMON O. LESSER, *Fiction and the Unconscious*. New York: Columbia University Press, 1957.

C. S. LEWIS, *An Experiment in Criticism*. Cambridge: Cambridge University Press, 1969.

DAVID LODGE, *Language of Fiction*. New York: Columbia University Press, 1966.

PERCY LUBBOCK, *The Craft of Fiction*. London: Jonathan Cape, 1921.

A. A. MENDILOW, *Time and the Novel*. London: P. Nevill, 1952.

J. HILLIS MILLER, *The Form of Victorian Fiction*. Notre Dame: University of Notre Dame Press, 1968.

EDWIN MUIR, *The Structure of the Novel*. New York: Harcourt Brace Jovanovich, 1928.

WILLIAM VAN O'CONNOR, ed., *Forms of Modern Fiction*. Bloomington: Indiana University Press, 1964.

JONATHAN RABAN, *The Techniques of Modern Fiction*. Notre Dame: University of Notre Dame Press, 1969.

ERIC S. RABKIN, *Narrative Suspense*. Ann Arbor: University of Michigan Press, 1973.

LOUIS D. RUBIN, JR., *The Teller in the Tale*. Seattle: University of Washington Press, 1967.

SHELDON SACKS, *Fiction and the Shape of Belief*. Berkeley: University of California Press, 1964.

ROBERT SCHOLES *and* ROBERT KELLOGG, *The Nature of Narrative*. New York: Oxford University Press, 1966.

ROBERT SCHOLES, ed., *Approaches to the Novel*. San Francisco: Chandler, 1961.

MARK SCHORER, *The World We Imagine*. New York: Farrar, Straus & Giroux, 1968.

SHARON SPENCER, *Space, Time and Structure in the Modern Novel*. New York: New York University Press, 1971.

MARK SPILKA, ed., *Toward a Poetics of Fiction*. Bloomington: Indiana University Press, 1977.

FRANZ STANZEL, *Narrative Situations in the Novel*. Bloomington: Indiana University Press, 1971.

PHILIP STEVICK, *The Chapter in Fiction*. Syracuse: Syracuse University Press, 1970.

KATHLEEN TILLOTSON, *The Tale and the Teller*. London: Rupert Hart-Davis, 1959.

WILLIAM YORK TINDALL, *The Literary Symbol*. Bloomington: Indiana University Press, 1960.

BORIS USPENSKY, *A Poetics of Composition.* Berkeley: University of California Press, 1973.

CHARLES CHILD WALCUTT, *Man's Changing Mask.* Minneapolis: University of Minnesota Press, 1966.

IAN WATT, *The Rise of the Novel.* Berkeley: University of California Press, 1957.

ARNOLD L. WEINSTEIN, *Vision and Response in Modern Fiction.* Ithaca: Cornell University Press, 1974.

Index

77 78 79 80 9 8 7 6 5 4 3 2 1